HARCOURT BRACE

Oo-pples and Boo-noo-noos

Songs and Activities for Phonemic Awareness

Hallie Kay Yopp • Ruth Helen Yopp

HARCOURT BRACE & COMPANY
ORLANDO ATLANTA AUSTIN BOSTON SAN FRANCISCO CHICAGO DALLAS NEW YORK
TORONTO LONDON

Phonic Awareness; copyright page

For permission to reprint copyrighted material, grateful acknowledgment is made to the following sources:

American Book Company: "I Make Myself Welcome" from *Meeting Music.* Lyrics copyright © 1966 by American Book Company.

Cherry Lane Music Publishing Company, Inc. (ASCAP): "Going to the Zoo" (Retitled: "Goin' to the Zoo") by Tom Paxton. Lyrics and music copyright © 1961, renewed 1989 by Cherry Lane Music Publishing Company, Inc. (ASCAP).

Dover Publications, Inc.: Music from "Hanstead Boys," folk song from Nova Scotia in *Songs and Ballads from Nova Scotia.*

Geordie Music Publishing Company: "Kitty Alone" by Jean Ritchie from *Children's Songs and Games from the Southern Mountains.* Lyrics and music copyright © 1964, 1978 by Jean Ritchie Geordie Music Publishing Company.

Harcourt Brace & Company: Adapted lyrics by Barbara Andress from "Hanstead Boys," folk song from Nova Scotia in *Songs and Ballads from Nova Scotia.* Adapted lyrics copyright © 1984 by Holt, Rinehart and Winston, Inc. "Whosery Here?" Kentucky folk song collected by Barbara Andress from *The Music Book,* Teacher's Reference Book, Kindergarten. Lyrics and music copyright © 1984 by Holt, Rinehart and Winston, Inc. Music by Barbara Andress from "His Four Fur Feet" by Margaret Wise Brown in *Holt Music* Teacher's Edition, Grade K. Music copyright © 1988 by Holt, Rinehart and Winston, Inc. "Little Arabella Miller" and "What Have You Seen?" from *Holt Music Rhythm and Tonal Reading Charts,* Teacher's Manual, by John Feierabend. Lyrics and music © 1989 by Holt, Rinehart and Winston, Inc. "Jennie Jenkins," Early American song from *The Music Book,* Teacher's Reference Book, Kindergarten. Lyrics and music copyright © 1984 by Holt, Rinehart and Winston, Inc. "Jig Jog Jig Jog" and "Barnyard Song," Kentucky Mountain folk song from *Holt Music,* Teacher's Edition, Grade K. Lyrics and music copyright © 1988 by Holt, Rinehart and Winston, Inc. "The Old Gray Horse" from *Holt Music,* Teacher's Edition, Grade 1. Lyrics and music copyright © 1988 by Holt, Rinehart and Winston, Inc. "Hocky Tocky Oombah" and "Jim Along, Josie" from *Holt Music,* Teacher's Edition, Grade 2. Copyright © 1988 by Holt, Rinehart and Winston, Inc.

Homeland Publishing, a division of Troubadour Records Ltd.: Adapted lyrics by Raffi and music by Larry Miyata in "Willoughby, Wallaby, Woo," from a poem by Dennis Lee. Adapted lyrics and music © 1976 by Homeland Publishing (SOCAN), a division of Troubadour Records Ltd. "The Corner Grocery Store," adapted lyrics by Raffi and D. Pike from *Raffi Children's Favorites.* Lyrics © 1979 by Homeland Publishing (SOCAN), a division of Troubadour Records Ltd.

Hyperion Books for Children: Lyrics from "His Four Fur Feet" in *Four Fur Feet* by Margaret Wise Brown. Lyrics copyright © 1961, renewed 1989 by Roberta Brown Rauch.

Little, Brown and Company: "Eletelephony" from *Tirra Lirra* by Laura E. Richards. Lyrics copyright 1930, 1932 by Laura E. Richards; lyrics copyright © renewed 1960 by Hamilton Richards.

Little Simon, an imprint of Simon & Schuster Children's Publishing Division: "Michael Finnegan," "Fooba-Wooba John," and "Old Molly Hare" from *The Fireside Book of Children's Songs,* collected and edited by Marie Winn, musical arrangements by Allan Miller. Lyrics and music copyright © 1966 by Marie Winn and Allan Miller; lyrics and music copyright renewed © 1994 by Marie Winn and Allan Miller. "Sarasponda," "Mary Had a William Goat," "The Kangaroo," and "Once an Austrian Went Yodeling" from *The Fireside Book of Fun and Game Songs,* collected and edited by Marie Winn, musical arrangements by Allan Miller. Lyrics and music copyright © 1974 by Marie Winn and Allan Miller.

Lothrop, Lee & Shepard Books, a division of William Morrow & Company, Inc.: Music by Jane Hart from "Eletelephony" by Laura Elizabeth Richards in *Singing Bee! A Collection of Favorite Children's Songs,* compiled by Jane Hart. Musical arrangement copyright © 1982 by Jane Hart.

Ludlow Music Inc., New York: "Howdido" by Woody Guthrie. Lyrics and music TRO - © copyright 1961 (renewed), 1964 (renewed) by Ludlow Music, Inc. "Little Sacka Sugar" by Woody Guthrie. Lyrics and music TRO - © copyright 1956 (renewed), 1963 (renewed) by Ludlow Music, Inc.

Oxford University Press: "The Frog in the Well," folk song from the Southern Appalachians, arranged by George Douglas from *English Folk Songs from the Southern Appalachians* by Cecil Sharp. Copyright by Oxford University Press.

Random House, Inc.: "Happy Birthday to Little Sally Spingel Spungel Sporn," "Somebody Stole My Hoo-To-Foo-To-Boo-To BAH!," and "Plinker Plunker Strummer Zummer Beeper Booper" from *The Cat in the Hat Songbook* by Dr. Seuss, piano score and guitar chords by Eugene Poddany. Lyrics and illustrations TM and copyright © 1967, renewed 1995 by Dr. Seuss Enterprises, L.P.; music copyright © 1967 by Eugene Poddany, renewed 1995 by Oleg Poddany.

Schocken Books, Inc.: "I've a Pair of Fishes" by J. Lillian Vandevere from *A Treasury of Jewish Folksongs,* edited by Ruth Rubin. Lyrics and music copyright © 1950 by Schocken Books, Inc., renewed 1978 by Ruth Rubin. Published by Pantheon Books, a division of Random House, Inc.

Silver Burdett Ginn, Simon & Schuster Elementary: "Burgalesa," folk song from Spain, English words by Verne Muñoz, arrangement by Francis Girard, and "A Ram Sam Sam," folk song from Morocco, from *Silver Burdett Music.* Lyrics and music © 1974 by Silver Burdett Ginn, Simon & Schuster Elementary. "The Pawpaw Patch," singing game from Kentucky, arrangement by Cameron McGraw, in *Making Music Your Own.* Lyrics and music © 1971 by Silver Burdett Ginn, Simon & Schuster Elementary.

Wadsworth Publishing Company, Inc.: "Clickety Clack" by Charles Harvey from *Singing with Children* by Robert and Vernice Nye, Neva Aubin, and George Kyme. Lyrics and music © 1962 by Wadsworth Publishing Company, Inc.

Walt Disney Music Company: "Bibbidi-Bobiddi-Boo," lyrics by Jerry Livingston, music by Mack David and Al Hoffman. Lyrics and music © 1948 by Walt Disney Music Company; lyrics and music copyright renewed.

Frederick Warne & Co., Inc.: "Lippity Lip!" by Dudley Glass from *The Songs of Peter Rabbit.* Lyrics and music copyright © 1951 by Frederick Warne & Co., Inc.

Warner Bros. Publications Inc., Miami, FL 33014: "The Name Game" by Lincoln Chase and Shirley Elliston. Lyrics and music © 1964 (renewed) by EMI Al Gallico Music Corp. and Embassy Music Corp. All rights for the U.S.A. administered jointly. All rights for the world outside the U.S.A. administered by EMI Al Gallico Music Corp.

Westwood Creative Artists: Lyrics from "Willoughby, Wallaby, Woo" in *Alligator Pie* by Dennis Lee. Lyrics copyright © 1974 by Dennis Lee. Published by Macmillan of Canada, 1974.

Printed in the United States of America ISBN 0-15-309028-6

8 9 10 076 99

A Note About the Authors

Dr. Hallie Kay Yopp is a professor in the Department of Elementary, Bilingual, and Reading Education at California State University in Fullerton, California. Her areas of expertise and special interest include phonemic awareness and early childhood education. In addition to her many publications and creative activities, she is a member of the author team for Harcourt Brace & Company, where she recently contributed to the development of the *Treasury of Literature* and *Signatures* Reading Programs.

Nationally known for her work in phonemic awareness, Dr. Hallie Kay Yopp has conducted many workshops for teacher and administrator groups. Attendees at these workshops, and others who have read her research, asked her to develop a sourcebook of phonemic awareness activities for teachers' use with their young students. This request led to the creation, with her twin sister, of this book, *Oo-pples and Boo-Noo-Noos: Songs and Activities for Phonemic Awareness.*

Dr. Ruth Helen Yopp is also a professor in the Department of Elementary, Bilingual, and Reading Education at California State University in Fullerton, California. Her areas of specialization and interest include literature-based reading programs and reading comprehension, and she has conducted workshops on reading development from early literacy to fluent reading across the curriculum. In addition, she coordinates the elementary credential program at the university and works extensively with beginning teachers. She is the author of numerous publications, and *Oo-pples and Boo-Noo-Noos: Songs and Activities for Phonemic Awareness* is the third book that she and her sister have co-authored.

CONTENTS

Page

Page

What Is Phonemic Awareness?

Phonemic awareness is, as the term suggests, an awareness of phonemes in the speech stream. It is the insight that speech consists of small units—phonemes; it is the understanding that larger units of speech (such as phrases or words) are made up of smaller units (phonemes). The spoken word *dog,* for instance, is made up of three sounds: */d/-/ŏ/-/g/.

Phonemic awareness can be difficult for young children because it demands a shift in attention from the *content* of speech to the *form* of speech. It requires individuals to attend to the sounds of speech separate from the meanings.

Individuals who are phonemically aware are able to do the following:

- rhyme
- blend isolated sounds together to form a word
- tell how many sounds can be heard in a word
- segment spoken words into their constituent sounds
- substitute sounds in spoken words
- add sounds to spoken words
- delete a sound from a spoken word

In other words, individuals who are phonemically aware are able to answer correctly the following questions:

Rhyme

Do these words rhyme?

fish—dish (yes)
hill—mail (no)
run—ran (no)

Phoneme Blending

What word do we have when we put these sounds together?

/ă/-/t/ (*at*)
/b/-/ĭ/-/g/ (*big*)
/ch/-/ĭ/-/n/ (*chin*)

*When letters appear between slashmarks (such as /d/), the sound rather than the letter name is represented.

Phoneme Counting

How many sounds do you hear in these words?

is (2)

book (3)

sit (3)

Phoneme Isolation

What is the beginning sound in *rose*? (/r/)

What is the final sound in *pencil*? (/l/)

What is the sound in the middle of *cat*? (/a/)

Phoneme Segmentation

What sounds do you hear in these words?

dog (/d/-/ŏ/-/g/)

race (/r/-/ā/-/s/)

up (/ŭ/-/p/)

Phoneme Substitution

What word would we have if we changed the /t/ in *Tommy* to an /m/? *(mommy)*

What word would we have if we changed the /t/ in *hot* to a /p/? *(hop)*

What word would we have if we changed the /i/ in *sit* to an /a/? *(sat)*

Phoneme Addition

What word would we have if we added /g/ to the beginning of *row*? *(grow)*

What word would we have if we added /l/ to the middle of *boo*? *(blue)*

What word would we have if we added /t/ to the end of *ow*? *(out)*

Phoneme Deletion

What word would we have if we left the /t/ out of the middle of *stand*? (*sand*)

What word would we have if we left the /s/ off the beginning of *spin*? *(pin)*

What word would we have if we left the /l/ off the end of *seal*? *(sea)*

Phonemic Awareness and Reading and Spelling Achievement

Research conducted during the last few decades has revealed that phonemic awareness is significantly related to success in learning to read and spell. The relationship is one of reciprocal causation or mutual facilitation. That is, phonemic awareness supports reading and spelling acquisition, and instruction in reading and spelling, in turn, supports further understanding of the phonemic basis of our speech. The relationship is so powerful that researchers have concluded the following:

- Phonemic awareness is the most potent predictor of success in learning to read. It is more highly related to reading than tests of general intelligence, reading readiness, and listening comprehension (Stanovich, 1986, 1994).
- The lack of phonemic awareness is the most powerful determinant of the likelihood of failure to learn to read (Adams, 1990).
- Phonemic awareness is the most important core and causal factor separating normal and disabled readers (Adams, 1990).
- Phonemic awareness is central in learning to read and spell (Ehri, 1984).

Why is phonemic awareness so important in learning to read and spell? Because English and other alphabetic languages map speech to print at the level of phonemes. In other words, our written language is a representation of the *sounds* of our spoken language. Therefore, it is critical to understand that our speech is made up of sounds. Without this insight, children have difficulty understanding the logic of the alphabetic system.

Fortunately, research suggests that phonemic awareness can be developed in individuals by providing them experiences with language that encourage active exploration and manipulation of sounds, and training studies reveal gains in phonemic awareness and in subsequent reading and spelling performance (Ball & Blachman, 1988; Bradley & Bryant, 1983; Cunningham, 1990; Lundberg, Frost & Peterson, 1988). Many researchers encourage preschool, kindergarten, and primary grade teachers to provide linguistically rich classroom environments where children are encouraged to play with the sounds of language (Adams, 1990; Griffith & Olson, 1992; Mattingly, 1984; Yopp, 1992).

Appropriate activities for young children have a sense of playfulness about them, are conducted in social settings that encourage interaction among children, pique children's curiosity about language and invite their experimentation with it, and allow for differences among children (Yopp, 1992).

This book includes many activities that are appropriate for young children. Provided here are verbal games, such as tongue twisters, jump-rope rhymes, and hink pinks; activities in which children manipulate objects that represent sounds; and books and songs that draw children's attention to the sounds of language. We hope that teachers find these valuable as they create linguistically stimulating environments for their students.

Word Play Activities

There is a wonderful oral tradition in which tongue twisters, counting-out chants, and jump-rope rhymes are passed from generation to generation and from one child to another. These verbal activities are excellent examples of children's (and adults') interest in and fascination with manipulating language. Some well-known tongue twisters, counting-out chants, and jump-rope rhymes, along with suggestions for other verbal games that focus on the manipulation of sounds, are provided in this section.

Tongue Twisters

Tongue twisters are phrases or sentences that are difficult to say fast, usually because of an alliteration or a sequence of nearly similar sounds that involves irregular patterns of sounds. Children enjoy the challenge of trying to articulate tongue twisters while at the same time—as they stumble over sounds—their consciousness of the phonological basis of language is being raised. Listed here are some common tongue twisters which may be used in whole or in part. Short tongue twisters (or, in some cases, the first line of longer tongue twisters) are appropriate for younger children; the object is to say them over and over again as quickly as possible. Older children may be able to master the longer tongue twisters, and saying them once all the way through is challenge enough.

Betty Botter bought some butter.
"But," she said, "the butter's bitter;
if I put it in my batter,
it will make my batter bitter.
But a bit of better butter—
that would make my batter better."

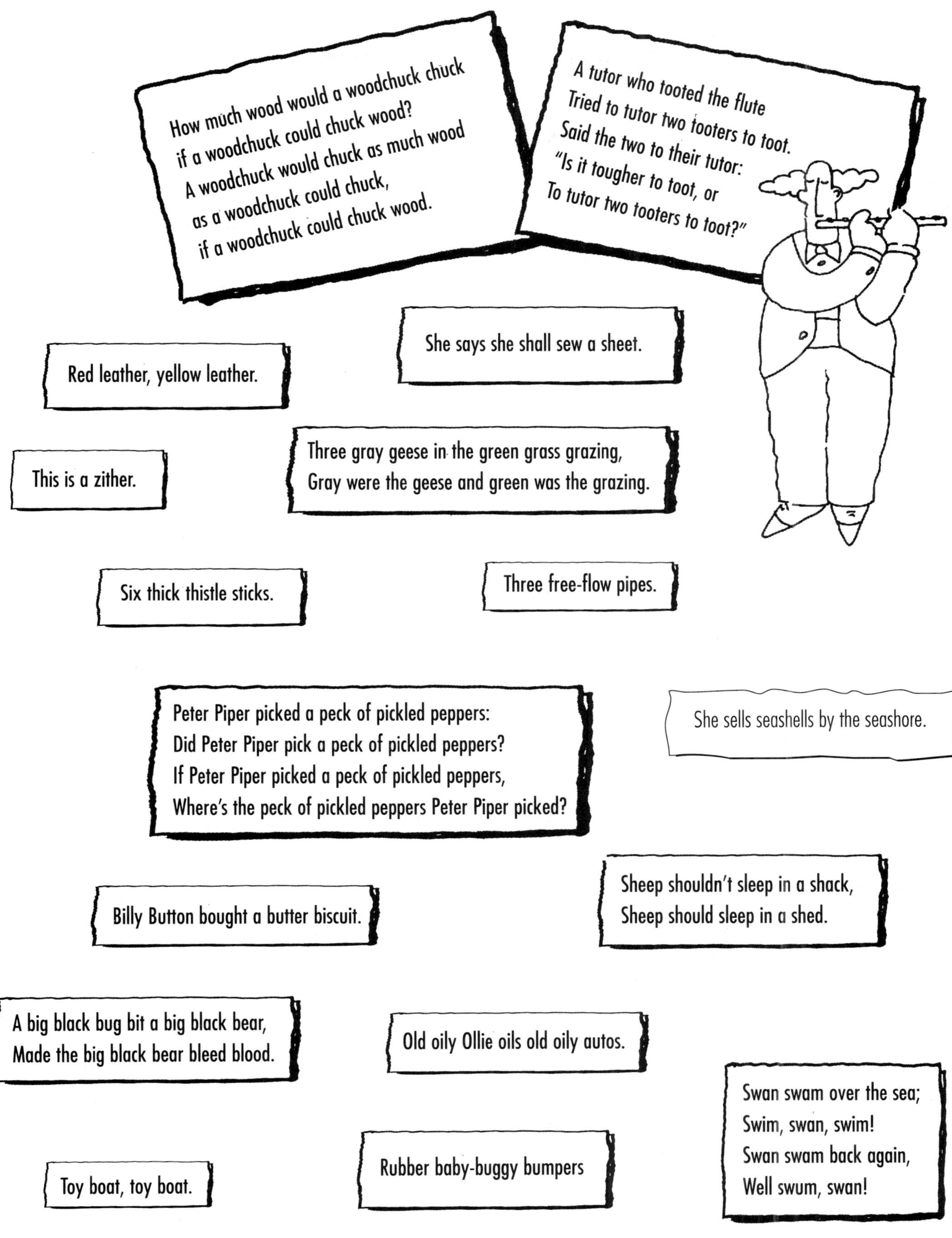
How much wood would a woodchuck chuck
if a woodchuck could chuck wood?
A woodchuck would chuck as much wood
as a woodchuck could chuck,
if a woodchuck could chuck wood.
A tutor who tooted the flute
Tried to tutor two tooters to toot.
Said the two to their tutor:
"Is it tougher to toot, or
To tutor two tooters to toot?"
She says she shall sew a sheet.
Red leather, yellow leather.
This is a zither.
Three gray geese in the green grass grazing,
Gray were the geese and green was the grazing.
Six thick thistle sticks.
Three free-flow pipes.
Peter Piper picked a peck of pickled peppers:
Did Peter Piper pick a peck of pickled peppers?
If Peter Piper picked a peck of pickled peppers,
Where's the peck of pickled peppers Peter Piper picked?
She sells seashells by the seashore.
Billy Button bought a butter biscuit.
Sheep shouldn't sleep in a shack,
Sheep should sleep in a shed.
A big black bug bit a big black bear,
Made the big black bear bleed blood.
Old oily Ollie oils old oily autos.
Swan swam over the sea;
Swim, swan, swim!
Swan swam back again,
Well swum, swan!
Toy boat, toy boat.
Rubber baby-buggy bumpers

Counting-Out Chants

Counting-out chants typically include rhyming nonsense words and patterns of sounds.

Inky, pinky, penny winky
Out goes she (*or* he).
Fireman, fireman, number eight.
Hit his head against the gate.
The gate flew in, the gate flew out.
That's the way he put the fire out.
O-U-T spells *out,* and out you go.
Acka backa soda cracker,
Acka backa boo,
Acka backa soda cracker,
Out goes you!
Oh, dear me,
Momma caught a flea.
Flea died, Momma cried,
One, two, three.
Ickle, ockle, bottle,
Ickle, ockle, out.
If you come to my house,
I will send you out.
O-U-T spells out,
And out you go for saying so.
My mother, your mother
Live across the way,
Every night they put out the light,
And this is what they say:
Hinky, dinky,
Soda crackers,
Hinky, dinky, boo,
Hinky, dinky,
Soda crackers,
Out goes you!

Jump-Rope Rhymes

Jump-rope rhymes, with their steady beat, often make use of nonsense words and rhyme patterns. Many of the rhymes we provide here are used also with ball bouncing.

12345...

Cinderella, dressed in yellow,
Went upstairs to kiss her fellow.
How many kisses did she get?
1, 2, 3, 4, 5, . . .

Cinderella, dressed in pink,
Washed her dishes in the kitchen sink.
How many dishes did she break?
1, 2, 3, 4, 5 . . .

Cinderella, dressed in red,
Went downtown to get some bread.
How many loaves did she buy?
1, 2, 3, 4, 5 . . .

This is the way you
spell *Tennessee:*
One a-see
Two a-see
Three a-see
Four a-see
Five a-see
Six a-see
Seven a-see
Eight a-see
Nine see
Tennessee

A my name is Alice (Adam),
My husband's (wife's) name is Adam (Alice).
We live in Alabama
And we sell apples.
B my name is Barbara (Bill),
My husband's (wife's) name is Bill (Barbara).
We live in Boston
And we sell beans.
C my name is . . .

(Children continue to invent each line, using successive letters of the alphabet.)

Bluebells, cockle shells,
Evie, Ivy, over,
Bluebells, cockle shells,
Evie, Ivy, under,
Bluebells, cockle shells,
Evie, Ivy, out.

Mother, Mother, I am sick.
Send for the doctor quick, quick, quick!
In came the doctor,
In came the nurse,
In came the lady with the alligator purse.
"Measles," said the doctor.
"Measles," said the nurse.
"Nothing," said the lady with the alligator purse.

Tick tock, tick tock.
Nine o'clock is striking.
Mother, may I go out?
All the kids are waiting.
One has an apple,
One has a bear,
One has a cookie,
One has a dollar . . .

(Children continue to invent each line, using successive letters of the alphabet.)

Two, four, six, eight
Meet me at the garden gate.
If you're late, I won't wait.
Two, four, six, eight.

Bubble gum, bubble gum in a dish
How many pieces do you wish?
1, 2, 3, 4, . . .

Not last night, but the night before
Twenty-four robbers came knockin' at my door.
As I ran out, they ran in.
I hit them on the head with a rolling pin.

I went downtown and met Miss Brown.
She gave me a nickel, I bought a pickle.
The pickle was sour, I bought a flower.
The flower was red, I bought some thread.
The thread was thin, I bought a pin.
The pin was sharp, I bought a harp.
And on that harp I played . . .

(This rhyme is used as a lead-in to any other rhyme.)

Pig Latin

Pig Latin is an excellent example of manipulation of sounds. The initial sound of each word is deleted and then added to the end of the word with an /ay/ sound. For instance, *nix* becomes *ix-nay, boy* becomes *oy-bay*, *teacher* becomes *eacher-tay,* and the name *Peter* becomes *Eter-pay.* Individuals who can speak rapid Pig Latin have considerable control over the phonemes of their speech.

Spoonerisms

Spoonerisms are named after the English clergyman William Spooner, who is thought to have made deliberate articulation errors in which initial sounds of words are substituted for one another as in "With this wing I thee red" or "I'd like a biece of pread."

Teachers can introduce spoonerisms to children and encourage children's attempts to create their own spoonerisms. A good way to introduce them is to use children's names. Children can switch the initial sounds in their first names and last names. *Randy Jones* becomes *Jandy Rones; Beth Hart* becomes *Heth Bart; Maria Tellez* becomes *Taria Mellez*.

Hink Pinks

Hink Pinks are pairs of words that rhyme, such as *sad lad, big pig,* and *high fly.* They are useful in focusing children's attention on the sounds of the words. Children can make up their own rhyming pairs of words or use clues to guess the word pair that someone else is thinking of. For example, what do you call an angry father? *A mad dad.* What do you call a humorous hare? *A funny bunny.*

The Guessing Game

Using a grab bag, picture cards, or their imaginations, children can give clues about what they have, what they see, or what they are thinking of. The teacher or a child slowly says the sounds of the name of an object and asks others to guess what it is. For example, the teacher may look into a grab bag and say, "I have a kind of toy. It is a /k/-/är/. Who knows what I have?" Children blend the sounds to discover that the toy is a car. Or, the teacher or a child may hold a card, with the picture on it hidden from view, and ask others to guess what the picture is. "It is an animal. It is a /f/-/ŏ/-/ks/ (fox)."

We have played this game with our own children on long car rides. "I'm thinking of something we'll see at the beach. It is a /sh/-/ĕ/-/l/." Our children shout out "shell!" and then take turns making up clues for the rest of us.

Name-Sound Substitutions

Some teachers focus on one particular letter at a time as they introduce the alphabet and sound/symbol correspondences. This is an opportune time to ask children to identify as many items in the classroom as they can that begin with that sound and then to substitute that sound into the initial position of other words. In emphasizing the letter *t*, for example, the teacher might ask children to name objects in the classroom that begin with /t/. Then they create new /t/ words by substituting /t/ for the initial sound of other objects; thus, a *chair* becomes a *tair* and a *desk* becomes a *tesk*. Names are especially salient to children. When /r/ is discussed, for example, all the children change their own names by using the /r/ sound at the beginning of their names so that *Billy* becomes *Rilly, Daniel* becomes *Raniel*, and *Isabel* becomes *Risabel*. Children can use their special new names for the entire day.

The Three Billy Goats

After children have read the story "The Three Billy Goats Gruff," they can reenact the story, varying the story line by including a phonemic awareness component in which the troll demands that the goats interpret a segmented code word in order to cross over the bridge. For example, the child or teacher taking the part of the troll might say, "Halt! What is this password? /g/-/r/-/ă/-/s/ (any word relevant to the story would do). A child who is one of the billy goats would respond "grass!" and so be permitted to pass. An alternative to the children reenacting the story is to have them construct a small bridge and use puppets.

Activities with Concrete Manipulation

Manipulating an object while manipulating sounds can help children develop an understanding of the nature of their speech. Each of the activities suggested here involves the use of blocks, counters, chips, or letters to represent sounds that are heard in speech.

Say It and Move It

In this activity described by Blachman (1991), children move the appropriate number of chips to represent the number of phonemes that are presented. Beginning with one sound, the teacher asks the child to move a chip for the sound, such as /ă/. The child moves one chip from a row at the top of the paper to the left end of an arrow drawn from left to right at the bottom of the paper (encouraging left-to-right directionality) and says the sound. The chip is returned to the top of the paper, and this activity is repeated for other sounds. "Move a chip for each sound you hear now—/f/." The child moves one chip to the arrow. "Move a chip for each sound you hear now—/b/." The child moves one chip.

/ă/

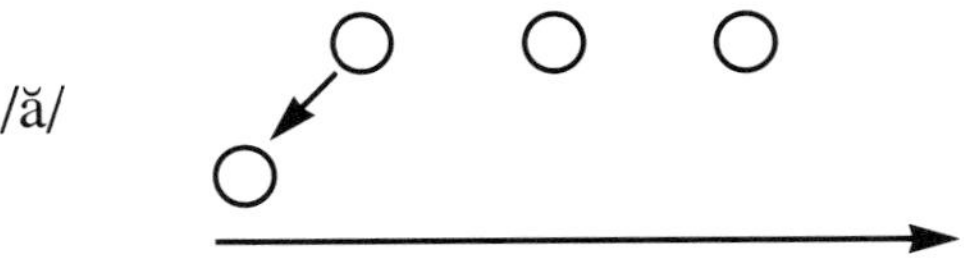

Then the teacher increases the number of phonemes presented, using the same sound twice initially. "Move a chip for each sound you hear now—/ĕ/ /ĕ/." The child repeats the sounds and moves a chip for each articulation, placing them on the arrow from left to right, one at a time. "Move a chip for each sound you hear now—/t/ /t/." The child moves two chips, one at a time, as he or she repeats the sounds.

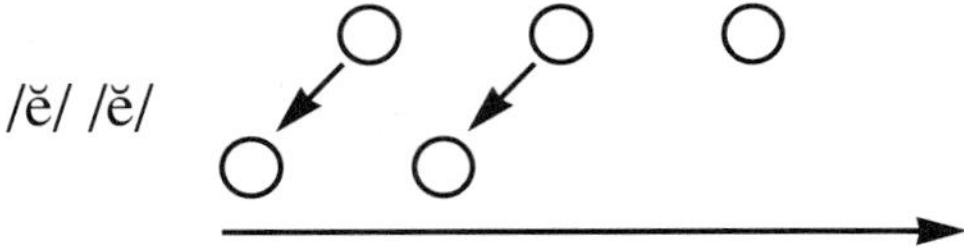

After the child is successful in representing repeated sounds with two chips, the teacher introduces two-phoneme and then three-phoneme words. "Move a chip for each sound you hear in the word *in*." The child moves a chip for /ĭ/ and a second chip for /n/. "Move a chip for each sound you hear in *man*." The child moves a chip for /m/, a chip for /ă/, and a chip for /n/.

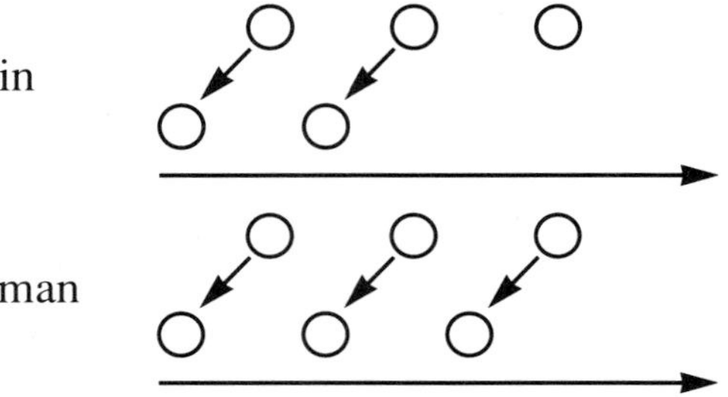

Elkonin Boxes

Designed by the Soviet educator Elkonin, this activity also provides children with experience segmenting the phonemes in words. As in the examples that follow, a simple drawing of a word to be analyzed is pictured above a set of boxes equal to the number of phonemes in the word. The children are asked to say the word represented by the picture and to move chips, coins, or counters into the boxes as they slowly say the word. In the first example, as the child slowly articulates the word *fish*, he or she puts a chip in the first box (on the left) and says /f/, a chip in the middle box and says /ĭ/, and a chip in the third box and says the sound /sh/. In the second example, the child moves a chip into the first box and says the /m/ in *mop*, a chip into the second box and says the /ŏ/, and a chip into the third box and says the /p/.

(fish)
(mop)
(clock)
(desk)
(nose)
(tree)
11
12
1
10
2
9
3
8
4
7
6
5

A variation of this activity is to have children move a chip representing a given sound into an initial, medial, or final box, depending upon the sound's position in a word. Thus, children are asked to focus on a phoneme's position in a word. For example, the teacher tells children to listen for the /m/ sound in the word *man* and then move a chip to the first, middle, or final box, depending on the sound's location, as they repeat the word.

Teacher: Say /m/. Listen for the /m/ in this word: *man*. Where is the /m/ sound in *man*?

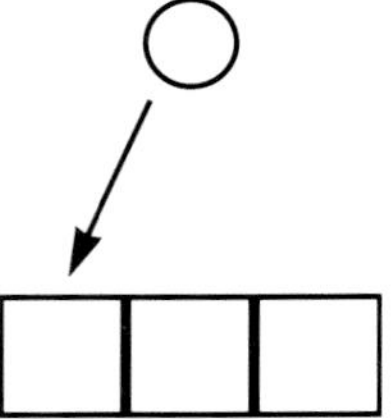

Teacher: Say /t/. Listen for the /t/ in this word: *hat*. Where is the /t/ sound in *hat*?

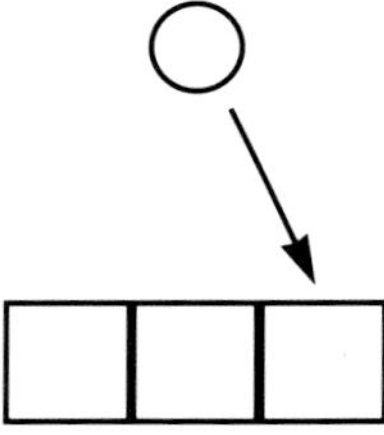

Teacher: Say /ŭ/. Listen for the /ŭ/ in this word: *bus*. Where is the /ŭ/ in *bus*?

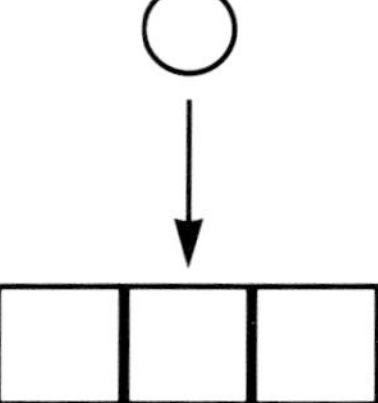

Making Words

Cunningham and Cunningham (1992) describe an activity they call Making Words in which children segment the phonemes of orally presented words and move small letter cards to represent the words in print. This activity builds awareness and an understanding of letter-sound mapping. It is appropriate for children who know some letter-sound correspondences.

For this activity, each child is given a set of cards with selected letters written on them. The children are asked to use the letters to build words, beginning with two-letter words and progressing to words with more and more letters, until they use all the letters in the set for a final word. For example, the children might be given the letter cards *a, l, n, p, s,* and *t.* (The Cunninghams suggest that the children line up their cards with the vowels first and then the consonants in alphabetical order.) Then, the teacher asks them to select the two cards that spell the word *an*. Children move the *a* and the *n* into position to spell the word. Then, the teacher asks them to change one letter to spell the word *at*. Next, she tells them to add one letter to spell the word *sat*. Children can be asked to spell the word *pat* and then to move the letters around to spell *tap*, highlighting that the order of letters in words is important. From there, children are asked to spell *taps, slap, pals, plan, pant, pants, plant*, and, finally, *plants*.

This activity draws attention to the sounds of words as children manipulate letter cards to spell the words. The Making Words activity can continue with the teacher using separate cards that display each of the words constructed in order to have children focus on certain patterns. For example, the teacher might want children to find all the words with /pl/, all the words that end with /t/, or the words that use /s/ to make plurals.

For a detailed description of this activity and many examples, see Cunningham and Cunningham in the October 1992 issue of *The Reading Teacher*.

Find the cards to spell the word *an*.

Change one letter to spell the word *at*.

Add one letter to make *sat*.

Change one letter to make *pat*.

Keep the letters but change their order to make *tap*.

Add a letter to make *taps*.

Now find new letters to spell *slap*.

Change the order of the letters to spell *pals*.

Change some letters to spell *plan*.

Spell *pant*.

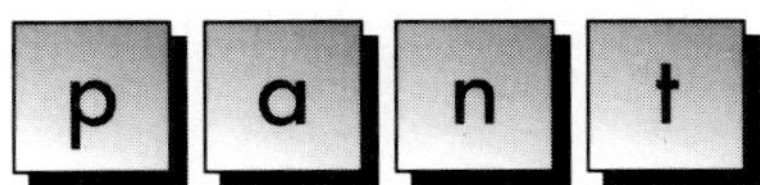

Add one letter to spell *pants*.

Has anyone figured out what word we can make with all our letters?

Read-Aloud Books That Develop Phonemic Awareness*

Read-aloud books serve as excellent vehicles for developing many literacy insights, including a sensitivity to the sound structure of language. Books that play with language by repeating sounds, mixing up sounds, substituting one sound for another, or making extensive use of rhyme help focus attention on sounds. Listed here are books that can be useful in helping children attend to the sounds of their language.

In each of these books, play with language is explicit and a critical, dominant feature. Thus, children are likely to notice the language that is used to communicate the message. And, the books lend themselves to further language play. Their patterns are explicit, their structures readily accessible, and their content simple enough that the stories can be extended by young children.

Books of this nature should be read over and over again. Teachers should encourage children to notice the language use, to have them make predictions, and tell how they derived their predictions. Generally, the answer will address the author's use of language. ("She's making the words rhyme!" "He's starting every word with the same sound!")

Follow-up activities can include having children compose additional verses to a poem, invent another version of a story, or engage in other activities that follow the pattern found in the text. For example, after listening to *The Hungry Thing,* children might construct their own Hungry Things, each one wearing a sign that says "FEED ME." Each child makes up something that his or her Hungry Thing wants to eat and the other children try to guess what it is: Erica says her Hungry Thing wants ricken and bice (chicken and rice); Thao says her Hungry Thing wants bapples and hoda (apples and soda).

After reading *There's a Wocket in My Pocket,* children can make their own books with drawings of unusual creatures in a setting of their choice: a classroom, their homes, the beach, a park, and so forth. Our sons' teacher read *Ten Cats Have Hats* and then had each child write and illustrate his or her own page for a classroom big book titled, "Twenty Kids Have Hats!" Gracie wrote, "One worm has germs, but I have a hat." Kelsi wrote, "Nine fishes have dishes, but I have a hat." Billy wrote, "Ten giraffes have calves, but I have a hat." Each page was followed by a painting each child did of himself or herself wearing a hat.

* Adapted from Yopp (1995a)

Annotated Bibliography

Brown, Margaret Wise. *Four Fur Feet.* Doubleday, 1993.

In this simple book, the reader is drawn to the /f/ sound: the phrase "four fur feet" is repeated in every sentence as a furry animal walks around the world. We see four fur feet walk along the river, into the country, and so forth. The book must be turned around as the animal makes its way around the world.

Buller, Jon & Schade, Susan. *I Love You, Good Night.* Simon & Schuster, 1988.

A mother and child tell each other how much they love one another. When the child says "as much as blueberry pancakes," the mother responds that she loves her child as much as "milkshakes." The child says she loves her mother as much as "frogs love flies," to which the mother responds she loves her *child* as much as "pigs love pies." The two go back and forth in this manner until good night is said. The rhyme invites the listener to participate and continue the story.

Cameron, Polly. *"I Can't." Said the Ant.* Coward-McCann, 1961.

Household items discuss the fall of a teapot from the counter in a kitchen and the means by which to put it back. In a series of brief contributions to the conversation, each item says something that rhymes with its own name. "'Don't break her,' said the shaker" and "'I can't bear it,' said the carrot."

Carle, Eric. *All About Arthur (An Absolutely Absurd Ape).* Franklin Watts, 1974.

Arthur, an accordion-playing ape who lives in Atlanta, feels lonely and travels from Baltimore to Yonkers making friends. In each city he makes a friend whose name matches the initial sound of the city—from a banjo-playing bear in Baltimore to a young yak in Yonkers.

Carter, David A. *More Bugs in Boxes.* Simon & Schuster, 1990.

In this pop-up book, the reader is presented with a series of questions and answers about make-believe bugs that are found inside a variety of boxes. Both the questions and answers make use of alliteration: "What kind of bug is in the rosy red rectangle box? A bright blue big-mouth bug." Following a similar pattern is the author's *Jingle Bugs* (1992, Simon & Schuster) which has a Christmas theme and makes use of rhyme: "Who's in the chimney, warm and snug? Ho, ho, ho! It's Santa Bug!"

de Regniers, Beatrice Schenk, Moore, E., White, M. & Carr, J. *Sing a Song of Popcorn.* Scholastic, 1988.

A number of poems in this book draw attention to rhyme and can be used to encourage children to experiment with rhyme. Also included are poems that play with sounds within words. In "Galoshes," the author describes the slippery slush "as it slooshes and sloshes and splishes and sploshes" around a child's galoshes. In "Eletelephony," sounds are mixed up and substituted for one another—" Once there was an elephant, Who tried to use the telephant—"

Deming, A.G. *Who Is Tapping at My Window?* Viking Penguin, 1994.

A young girl hears a tap-tapping at her window and asks who is there. The farm animals each respond "It's not I" and she discovers that it is the rain. The book is predictable in that each pair of animals rhyme. The loon responds, followed by the raccoon. The dog's response is followed by the frog's.

Ehlert, Lois. *Eating the Alphabet: Fruits and Vegetables from A to Z.* Harcourt Brace, 1989.

Fruits and vegetables are offered in print and pictures for each letter of the alphabet in this book. The following are displayed for B, for instance: blueberry, brussel sprouts, bean, beet, broccoli, banana.

Eichenberg, Fritz. *Ape in a Cape.* Harcourt Brace, 1980.

In this alphabet book of odd animals, we meet an ape in a cape, a pig in a wig, a rat with a bat, and others. The original publication was named a Caldecott Honor Book.

Emberley, Barbara. *One Wide River to Cross.* Little, Brown, 1992.

This Caldecott Honor Book is a picture book adaptation of the traditional African-American spiritual about Noah's ark. Through the use of rhyme, the author describes the animals gathering on board one by one (while "Japhelth played the big bass drum"), two by two ("The alligator lost his shoe"), and so on up to ten, when the rains begin.

Fortunata. *Catch a Little Fox.* Scholastic, 1968.

In this repetitious book, children talk about going hunting. One by one they identify animals they will catch and where they will keep each one. A frog will be put in a log, a cat will be put in a hat, and so forth. The story concludes with the animals capturing the children, putting them in a ring and listening to them sing. Then they are released. The music is included in this book. A different version of this story that includes a brontosaurus (who is put in a chorus) and an armadillo (who is put in a pillow) is J. Langstaff's (1974) *Oh, A-Hunting We Will Go* published by Atheneum.

Galdone, Paul. *Cat Goes Fiddle-i-fee.* Clarion, 1985.

This is the old English rhyme that tells the story of a boy feeding his farm animals. As the animals are fed, they make noises: pig goes guffy guffy, the cat goes fiddle-i-fee, and the hen goes chimmy-chuck, chimmy-chuck. Sound repetition is a dominant part of this book.

Galdone, Paul. *Henny Penny.* Scholastic, 1968.

A hen becomes alarmed when an acorn hits her on the head. She believes the sky is falling, and on her way to inform the king she meets several animals who join her until they all get eaten by Foxy Loxy. This classic story is included here because of the amusing rhyming names of the animals. A more recent release of this story is Steven Kellogg's *Chicken Little* (1985) published by Mulberry Books, 1992.

Geraghty, Paul. *Stop That Noise!* Crown, 1992.

A mouse is annoyed with the many sounds of the forest and implores the cicada to stop its "zee-zee-zee-zee," the frog to stop is "woopoo," until it hears far more disturbing sounds—the "Brrrm" and "Crrrrrr RACKA-DACKA-RACKA-SHOONG" of a bull-dozer felling trees. The presentation of animal and machine sounds make this book useful in drawing attention to the sounds in our language.

Gilman, P. *The Wonderful Pigs of Jillian Jiggs.* Scholastic, 1993.

"Jillian Jillian Jillian Jiggs, Maker of wonderful, marvelous pigs!" In this rhyming book, a young girl enthusiastically makes pigs to sell. When she realizes that she cannot part with them, she teaches others how to make them. Instructions for making pigs are included for the reader.

Gordon, Jeffie Ross. *Six Sleepy Sheep.* Puffin Books, 1991.

Six sheep try to fall asleep by slurping celery soup, telling spooky stories, singing songs, sipping simmered milk and so on. The use of the /s/ sound is prevalent throughout and amuses listeners as they anticipate the sheep's antics.

Hague, K. *Alphabears.* Henry Holt, 1984.

In this beautifully illustrated book, 26 teddy bears introduce the alphabet and make use of alliteration. Teddy bear John loves jam and jelly. Quimbly is a quilted bear and Pam likes popcorn and pink lemonade.

Hawkins, Colin & Jacqui. *Tog the Dog.* G.P. Putnam's Sons, 1986.

This books tells the story of Tog the Dog who likes to jog, gets lost in a fog, falls into a bog, and so forth. Emphasis is on words that rhyme with dog. With the exception of the final page, the pages in the book are not full width. On the final page the letters "og" appear in large bold type. As the reader turns the narrower pages throughout the text a new letter appears and lines up with the "og"—thus a new word is presented on each page. When Tog falls into the bog, a large letter "b" lines up with the "og" to make the word, "bog." This is a great book for both developing phonemic awareness and pointing out a spelling pattern. Also by the authors are *Jen the Hen, Mig the Pig,* and *Pat the Cat.*

Hymes, Lucia & Hymes, James. *Oodles of Noodles.* Young Scott Books, 1964.

Several of the poems in this collection make use of nonsense words in order to complete a rhyme. In the poem "Oodles of Noodles," the speaker requests oodles of noodles because they are his/her favorite foodles. In a poem entitled "Spinach," the authors list a series of words each beginning with the /sp/ sound until they finally end with the word "spinach." Words include "spin," "span," "spun," and "spoony." Many of the other poems point out spelling patterns, and these will be entertaining to an older audience.

Krauss, Ruth. *I Can Fly.* Golden Press, 1958.

In this simple book, a child imitates the actions of a variety of animals. "A cow can moo. I can too." "I can squirm like a worm." "Howl howl howl I'm an old screech owl." The rhyming element combined with the charm of the child's imaginative play is what makes the story so engaging. On the final page, nonsense words that rhyme are used, encouraging listeners to experiment with sounds themselves: "Gubble, gubble gubble I'm a mubble in a pubble."

Kuskin, Karla. *Roar and More.* HarperTrophy, 1990.

This book includes many poems and pictures that portray the sounds that a variety of animals make. Both the use of rhyme and presentation of animal sounds ("Ssnnaaaarrll" for the tiger, "Hssssss . . ." for the snake) draw children's attention to sounds. An earlier edition of this book won the 1979 NCTE Award for Excellence in Poetry for Children.

Lewison, Wendy C. *Buzz Said the Bee.* Scholastic, 1992.

A series of animals sit on top of one another in this story. Before each animal climbs on top of the next it does something that rhymes with the animal it approaches. For instance, the hen dances a jig before sitting on the pig. The pig takes a bow before sitting on the cow.

Lindbergh, Reeve. *The Day the Goose Got Loose.* Viking Penguin, 1990.

Chaos results when a goose gets loose in this rhyming book. The horses were glad; they ran like mad. Mom was upset because the goose was a pet. The sheep were scared; they huddled and stared.

Martin, Bill, Jr. *The Happy Hippopotami.* Voyager Books, Harcourt Brace, 1991. Text copyright by Holt, Rinehart, and Winston, 1970.

This clever book makes use of rhyme and phoneme substitution as happy hippopotamamas wearing pretty beach pajamas and happy hippopotapoppas strolling about the candy shoppas have fun with family and friends at the beach.

Martin, Bill, Jr. *Sounds of a Powwow.* Holt, Rinehart, Winston, 1974.

Included in this volume is the song K-K-K-Katy in which the first consonant of several words is isolated and repeated, as in the song title. This song presents the opportunity for teachers to work with children on segmenting the sounds of their language.

Martin, Bill, Jr. and Archambault, John. *Listen to the Rain.* Henry Holt, 1988.

This delightful book plays with language as the authors describe the rain, "Leaving all outdoors a muddle, a mishy, mushy, muddy puddle" and "The tiptoe pitter-patter, the splish and splash and splatter," making use of rhyme and medial sound substitution.

Martin, Bill, Jr. and Archambault, John. *Chicka Chicka Boom Boom.* Scholastic, 1989.

The letters of the alphabet meet at the top of the coconut tree. Rhyme and silly play with sounds ("Skit skat skoodle doot. Flip flop flee.") make this book a must for preschool, kindergarten, and first grade teachers.

Martin, Bill, Jr. and Egielski, R. *"Fire! Fire!" Said Mrs. McGuire.* Harcourt Brace, 1971.

In this version of the well-known rhyme in which everyone's name rhymes with an exclamation for help, the fire is caused by the many candles on a birthday cake. The text is accompanied by colorful and often humorous illustrations.

Marzollo, J. *The Teddy Bear Book.* Dial, 1989.

Poems about teddy bears that the author adapted from songs, jump-rope rhymes, ball bouncing chants, cheers, and story poems are presented. Use of rhyme is considerable, from the well known, "Teddy bear, teddy bear, turn around, Teddy bear, teddy bear, touch the ground" to the less familiar, "Did you ever, ever, ever see a teddy bear dance with his wife" and the response, "No I never, never, never . . ." Play with sounds is obvious in the poem "Teddy Boo and Teddy Bear" where the author says, "Icabocker, icabocker, icabocker, boo! Icabocker, soda cracker, phooey on you!"

Marzollo, J. *Ten Cats Have Hats.* Scholastic, 1994.

A young child proudly shows a different hat on each page of this counting book as she tells the possessions of others: "Five ducks have trucks, but I have a hat," "Eight crabs have cabs, but I have a hat." The story is predictable, beginning with one bear and ending with ten cats, and makes obvious use of rhyme.

McDonald, Amy. *Rachel Fister's Blister.* Houghton Mifflin, 1990.

Rachel Fister gets a blister on her little toe. Her family enlists the aid of many people ("Find her brothers and some others . . ." "Call the palace. Ask Queen Alice . . .") and finally discovers that her mother's kiss makes the pain disappear.

Moerbeek, K. *Can't Sleep.* Price Stern Sloan, 1994.

In this highly repetitive pop-up book, a number of animals have difficulty sleeping because they think they are being watched. The /w/ sound is repeated more and more on each page as the fear mounts until the vulture shrieks, "Somebody is w-w-w-w-watching me!" The iteration of the /w/ and the elongation of the /s/ sound when a snake ssssighs focus attention on sounds in this story.

Most, Bernard. *Cock-a-Doodle-Moo!* Harcourt Brace, 1996.

A rooster discovers that it has lost its voice one morning and is unable to awaken everyone on the farm. Learning of the problem, a cow attempts to help but can't say "cock-a-doodle-doo" quite right. The resulting sound gives everyone an early morning laugh. This book makes use of phoneme addition and phoneme substitution and is a natural for developing a child's awareness of sounds.

Obligado, Lilian. *Faint Frogs Feeling Feverish and Other Terrifically Tantalizing Tongue Twisters.* Viking Penguin, 1983.

For each letter of the alphabet, one or more tongue twisters using alliteration are presented in print and with humorous illustrations. "S" has smiling snakes sipping strawberry sodas, a shy spider spinning, and a swordfish sawing. "T" presents two toucans tying ties, turtles tasting tea, and tigers trying trousers.

Ochs, Carol. P. *Moose on the Loose.* Carolrhoda, 1991.

A moose escapes from the zoo in the town of Zown and at the same time a chartreuse caboose disappears. The zookeeper runs throughout the town asking citizens if they've seen a "moose on the loose in a chartreuse caboose." No one has seen the moose, but each has seen a different animal. Included among the many citizens is Ms. Cook who saw a pig wearing a wig, Mr. Wu who saw a weasel paint at an easel, and Mrs. Case who saw a skunk filling a trunk. Each joins in the search.

Otto, Carolyn B. *Dinosaur Chase.* HarperTrophy, 1991.

A mother dinosaur reads her young one a story about dinosaurs in which "dinosaur crawl, dinosaur creep, tiptoe dinosaur, dinosaur sneak." Both alliteration and rhyme are present in this simple, colorful book.

Parry, Caroline. *Zoomerang-a-Boomerang: Poems to Make Your Belly Laugh.* Puffin, 1991.

Nearly all of the works included in this collection of poems play with language, particularly through the use of predictable and humorous rhyme patterns. In "Oh my, no more pie," the meat's too red so the writer has some bread. When the bread is too brown, the writer goes to town, and so forth. In "What they said," each of twelve animals says something that rhymes with the type of animal it is. For instance, a pup says "Let's wake up," and a lark says, "It's still dark." This pattern is similar to that presented in *"I Can't," Said the Ant.*

Patz, Nancy. *Moses Supposes His Toeses Are Roses.* Harcourt Brace, 1983.

Seven rhymes are presented here, each of which plays on language to engage the listener. Rhyme is predictable in "Sweetie Maguire" when she shouts "Fire! Fire!" and Mrs. O'Hair says, "Where? Where?" Alliteration makes "Betty Botter" a tongue twister: "But a bit of better butter—that will make my batter better!" Assonance adds humor to "The tooter" when a tooter tries to tutor two tooters to toot!

Pomerantz, Charlotte. *If I Had a Paka.* Mulberry, 1993.

A selection of twelve poems is included in this volume, and eleven languages are represented. The author manipulates words as in "You take the blueberry, I'll take the dewberry. You don't want the blueberry, OK Take the bayberry . . ." Many berries are mentioned, including a novel one—the "chuckleberry." Attention is drawn to phonemes when languages other than English are introduced. The Vietnamese translation of the following draws attention to rhyme and repetition: I like fish, Toy tik ka; I like chicken, Toy tik ga; I like duck, Toy tik veet; I like meat, Toy tik teet."

Prelutsky, Jack. *The Baby Uggs Are Hatching.* Mulberry, 1982.

Twelve poems describe unusual creatures such as the sneepies, the smasheroo, and the numpy-numpy-numpity. Though some of the vocabulary gets advanced (the Quossible has an irascible temper), most of the poems will be enjoyed by young children who will delight in the humorous use of words and sounds. For instance, "The Sneezysnoozer sneezes in a dozen sneezy sizes, it sneezes little breezes and it sneezes big surprises." In the poem which lends its name to the title of the book, children will hear sounds manipulated in nonsense words: "Uggily wuggily zuggily zee, and baby Uggs are fierce and free. Uggily wuggily zuggily zay, the baby Uggs come out today."

Prelutsky, Jack. *Poems of A. Nonny Mouse.* Knopf. 1989.

A. Nonny Mouse finally gets credit for all her works that were previously attributed to "Anonymous" in this humorous selection of poems that is appropriate for all ages. Of particular interest for developing phonemic awareness are poems such as "How much wood would a woodchuck chuck" and "Betty Botter bought some butter."

Provensen, Alice & Martin. *Old Mother Hubbard.* Random House, 1977.

In this traditional rhyme, Old Mother Hubbard runs errand after errand for her dog. When she comes back from buying him a wig, she finds him dancing a jig. When she returns from buying him shoes, she finds him reading the news. The rhyme element is a critical feature of this story.

Raffi. *Down by the Bay.* Crown, 1987.

In this story two young children try to outdo one another in making up rhymes with questions like, "Did you ever see a goose kissing a moose?" and "Did you ever see a bear combing his hair?" Music is included.

Raffi. *Tingalayo.* Crown, 1989.

Another of Raffi's songs is made into a book. Here the reader meets a man who calls for his donkey, Tingalayo, and describes its antics through the use of rhyme and rhythm. Phrases such as "Me donkey dance, me donkey sing, me donkey wearin' a diamond ring" will make children laugh.

Rosen, Michael J. *Poems for the Very Young.* Kingfisher Books, 1993.

The author provides us with a selection of poems sure to engage young listeners. Many make use of rhyme ("Goodness gracious, fiddle dee dee, Somebody's grandmother out to sea). Some make use of alliteration ("Lily likes lollipops, lemonade and lime-drops"). Some make nonsensical play with sounds ("whipper-snapper, rooty-tooty, Helter-skelter, tutti-frutti").

Sendak, Maurice. *Alligators All Around: An Alphabet.* HarperTrophy, 1990.

Using alliteration for each letter of the alphabet, Sendak introduces the reader to the alphabet with the help of alligators who have headaches (for H) and keep kangaroos (for K).

Seuss, Dr. *Dr. Seuss's ABC.* Random House, 1963.

Each letter of the alphabet is presented along with an amusing sentence in which nearly all of the words begin with the targeted letter. "Many mumbling mice are making midnight music in the moonlight . . . mighty nice."

Seuss, Dr. *Fox in Socks.* Random House, 1965.

Before beginning this book the reader is warned to take the book slowly because the fox will try to get the reader's tongue in trouble. The play with language is the very obvious focus of this book. Assonance patterns occur throughout, and the listener is exposed to vowel sound changes when beetles battle, ducks like lakes, and ticks and clocks get mixed up with the chicks and tocks.

Seuss, Dr. *There's a Wocket in My Pocket.* Random House, 1974.

A child talks about the creatures he has found around his house. These include a "nooth grush on my tooth brush" and a "zamp in the lamp." The initial sounds of common household objects are substituted with other sounds to make the nonsense creatures. A wonderful example of play with language!

Shaw, Nancy. *Sheep on a Ship.* Houghton Mifflin, 1989.

Sheep sailing on a ship run into trouble when facing a sudden storm. This entertaining story makes use of rhyme (waves lap and sails flap), alliteration (sheep on a ship), and assonance ("It rains and hails and shakes the sails"). Also by this author are *Sheep in a Jeep, Sheep Out to Eat,* and *Sheep Take a Hike.*

Shelby, Anne. *Potluck.* Orchard, 1991.

Two friends, Alpha and Betty, organize a potluck and each of their friends contribute something. Christine came with carrot cake and corn on the cob. Monica made mounds and mounds of mashed potatoes. Alliteration draws attention to initial sounds throughout this book.

Showers, Paul. *The Listening Walk.* HarperTrophy, 1991.

A girl and her father go for a walk with their dog, and the listener is treated to the variety of sounds they hear while walking. These include "thhhhh . . . ," the steady whisper sound of some sprinklers and "whithh whithh," the sound of other sprinklers that turn around and around. Some phonemes are elongated as in "eeeeeeeyowwwoooo . . . ," the sound of a jet overhead. Some phonemes are substituted as in "bik bok bik bok," the sounds of high heels on the pavement.

Silverstein, Shel. *Falling Up.* HarperCollins, 1996.

Few children will not be entertained by the poetry of Shel Silverstein. In his latest collection there are many selections that play with sounds. For example, "My Nose Garden" begins, "I have rowses and rowses of noses and noses, And why they all growses I really can't guess." Sound substitution, sound repetition and rhyme abound in these humorous and occasionally poignant poems.

Silverstein, Shel. *A Giraffe and a Half.* HarperCollins, 1964.

Using cumulative and rhyming patterns, Silverstein builds the story of a giraffe who has a rose on his nose, a bee on his knee, some glue on his shoe, and so on until he undoes the story by reversing the events.

Slepian, Jan. & Seidler, A. *The Hungry Thing.* Scholastic, 1967.

One day a Hungry Thing shows up in town. Only a little boy can understand what the Hungry Thing would like to eat when the creature tells the townspeople he wants shmancakes. Shmancakes, says the little boy, "sound like Fancakes . . . sound like . . . Pancakes to me." Using sound substitution, the authors develop a clever tale in which the townspeople must play with sounds in common words ("boop with a smacker" is "soup with a cracker") in order to communicate with the Hungry Thing. Two other Hungry Thing books are: *The Hungry Thing Returns* and *The Hungry Thing Goes to a Restaurant.*

Staines, Bill. *All God's Critters Got a Place in the Choir.* Viking Penguin, 1989.

This lively book makes use of rhyme to tell of the place that numerous animals—an ox and a fox, a grizzly bear, a possum and a porcupine, bullfrogs—have in the world's choir. "Some sing low, some sing higher, some sing out loud on the telephone wire."

Tallon, Robert. *Zoophabets.* Scholastic, 1979.

Letter by letter, the author names a fictional animal and in list form tells where it lives and what it eats. All, of course, begin with the targeted letter. "Runk" lives in "Rain barrels" and eats "raindrops, rusty rainbows, ripped rubbers, raincoats, rhubarb."

Van Allsburg, Chris. *The Z was Zapped.* Houghton Mifflin, 1987.

A series of mishaps befalls the letters of the alphabet. "A" is crushed by an avalanche, "B" is bitten badly, "C" is cut to ribbons, and so forth. Other alphabet books using alliteration include G. Base's *Animalia* (1987) published by Harry N. Abrams, K. Greenaway's (1993) *A Apple Pie* published by Derrydale, and J. Patience's (1993) *An Amazing Alphabet* published by Random House.

West, Colin. *"I Don't Care!" Said the Bear.* Candlewick, 1996.

A cocky bear (with his nose in the air) is not afraid of a loose moose, a big pig, a snake from a lake, or other such animals, but he runs from the teeny weeny mouse. Rhyme is used throughout this book.

Winthrop, E. *Shoes.* HarperTrophy, 1986.

This rhyming book surveys many familiar and some not-so-familiar types of shoes. The book begins, "There are shoes to buckle, shoes to tie, shoes too low, and shoes too high." Later we discover, "Shoes for fishing, shoes for wishing, rubber shoes for muddy squishing." This rhythm and rhyme book invites participation and creative contributions.

Wood, Audrey. *Silly Sally.* Harcourt Brace, 1992.

Rhyme and alliteration are obvious is this book about Silly Sally who goes to town and makes some acquaintances along the way. She does a jig with a pig, plays leapfrog with a dog, and sings a tune with a loon.

Zemach, Margot. *Hush, Little Baby.* E. P. Dutton, 1976.

In this lullaby, parents attempt to consol a crying baby by promising a number of outrageous things including a mockingbird, a diamond ring, a billy goat, and cart and bull. The verse is set to rhyme, e. g., "If that cart and bull turn over, Poppa's gonna buy you a dog name Rover," and children can easily innovate on the rhyme and contribute to the list of items being promised.

BIBLIOGRAPHY

Adams, M.J. (1990). *Beginning to Read: Thinking and Learning About Print.* Cambridge, MA: MIT Press.

Arnold, A. (1964). *The Big Book of Tongue Twisters and Double Talk.* New York: Random House.

Ball, E. & Blachman, B. (1988). Phoneme segmentation training: Effect on reading readiness. *Annals of Dyslexia, 38,* 208–225.

Blachman, B. (1991). *Getting Ready to Read. Learning How Print Maps to Speech.* Washington, D. C.: U.S. Department of Health and Human Services.

Bradley, L. & Bryant, P. (1983). Categorizing sounds and learning to read—a causal connection. *Nature, 301,* 419–421.

Clark, H.H. & Clark, E.V. (1977). *Psychology and Language.* New York: Harcourt Brace Jovanovich.

Cole, J. (1989). *Anna Banana.* New York: A Beechtree Paperback Book.

Cunningham, A.E. (1990). Explicit versus implicit instruction in phonemic awareness. *Journal of Experimental Child Psychology, 50,* 429–444.

Cunningham, P., & Cunningham, J. (1992). Making words: enhancing the invented spelling-decoding connection. *The Reading Teacher, 46(2),* 106–115.

Emrich, D. (1970). *The Nonsense Book.* New York: Four Winds Press.

Ehri, L. (1984). The development of spelling knowledge and its role in reading acquisition and reading dsisability. *Journal of Learning Disabilities, 22,* 356–365.

Geller, L.G. (1983). Children's rhymes and literacy learning: Making connections. *Language Arts, 60,* 184–193.

Geller, L.G. (1982a). Grasp of meaning: Theory into practice. *Language Arts, 59,* 571–579.

Geller, L.G. (1982b). Linguistic consciousness-raising: Child's play. *Language Arts, 59,* 120–125.

Griffith, P.L & Olson, M.W. (1992). Phonemic awareness helps beginning readers break the code. *The Reading Teacher, 45(7),* 516–523.

Loredo, E. (1996). *The Jump Rope Book.* New York: Workman.

Lundberg, I.; Frost, J.; & Peterson, O. (1988). Effects of an extensive program for stimulating phonological awareness in preschool children. *Reading Research Quarterly, 23,* 263–284.

Mattingly, I. (1984). Reading, linguistic awareness, and language acquisition. In J. Downing & R. Caltin (Eds.), *Language Awareness and Learning to Read* (pp. 9–25). New York: Springer-Verlag.

Stanovich, K.E. (1986). Matthew effects in reading: Some consequences of individual differences in the acquisition of literacy. *Reading Research Quarterly, 21,* 360–407.

Stanovich, K.E. (1994). Romance and reality. *The Reading Teacher, 47(4),* 280–291.

Yopp, H.K. (1988). The validity and reliability of phonemic awareness tests. *Reading Research Quarterly, 23,* 159–177.

Yopp, H.K. (1992). Developing phonemic awareness in young children. *The Reading Teacher, 45(9),* 696–703.

Yopp, H.K. (1995a). Read-aloud books for developing phonemic awareness: An annotated bibliography. *The Reading Teacher, 48,* 538-542.

Yopp, H.K. (1995b). A test for assessing phonemic awareness in young children. *The Reading Teacher, 49(1),* 20–29.

Songs That Play with Sounds

Young children enjoy singing. Some songs are especially useful for promoting an awareness of sounds and experimentation with and manipulation of language. Songs that are alliterative or make extensive use of rhyme demand attention to sounds. Songs in which there is phoneme substitution or addition help build an awareness that phonemes within words can be manipulated. Songs that make use of nonsensical combinations of sounds draw children's attention to the sound basis rather than the meaning basis of the lyrics. Included here are many songs that can be useful in promoting phonemic awareness. These songs may be sung as written or the teacher may encourage children to play with the lyrics by adding or changing verses or by substituting sounds. For, instance, instead of singing "Willoughby, Wallaby, Woo," children might sing "Lilloughby, Lallaby, Loo." Many well-known children's songs that are not included in this volume are good candidates for sound manipulation. For example, in "Old MacDonald Had a Farm" the phrase E-I-E-I-O can be changed by adding phonemes: Be-Bi-Be-Bi-Bo or He-Hi-He-Hi-Ho. In "I've Been Working on the Railroad," teachers can encourage children to substitute phonemes in the phrase "Fee-Fi-Fiddlee-I-O" to sing "Kee-Ki-Kiddlee-I-O" or "See-Si-Siddlee-I-O."

On the following pages is a chart listing each of the songs included in this volume, identified by type of phonemic manipulation (i.e., rhyme, alliteration, phoneme substitution, phoneme addition, or nonsense manipulation of phonemes).

Music is a wonderful medium for encouraging children to continue their learning, as singing can "spill over" from the classroom onto the playground and into children's homes.

Planning Guide

Oo-pples and Boo-noo-noos: Songs and Activities for Phonemic Awareness and the *Oo-pples and Boo-noo-noos Audiocassette* can be used to foster phonemic awareness. This chart lists the songs in this book and the skill(s) that each can be used to develop.

Song	Rhyme	Alliteration	Phoneme Substitution	Phoneme Addition	Nonsense Manipulation
Apples and Bananas			●		
A Ram Sam Sam					●
Barnyard Song	●	●			
Bibbidi-Bobbidi-Boo		●	●		●
Burgalesa				●	
Clickety-Clack	●	●	●		
The Corner Grocery Store	●				
Down By the Bay	●				
Eletelephony	●		●		
Fooba-Wooba John	●		●		
The Frog in the Well	●	●	●		●
Goin' to the Zoo	●	●	●		
Hanstead Boys	●				
Happy Birthday to Little Sally Spingel Spungel Sporn	●	●			
His Four Fur Feet		●		●	
Hocky Tocky Oombah			●		●
Howdido		●	●		●
I Make Myself Welcome	●	●			

Song	Rhyme	Alliteration	Phoneme Substitution	Phoneme Addition	Nonsense Manipulation
I've a Pair of Fishes	●			●	
Jennie Jenkins	●	●	●		●
Jig Jog Jig Jog	●	●	●		●
Jim Along, Josie		●			
The Kangaroo	●	●			●
Kitty Alone	●	●			●
Lippity Lip	●	●	●		
Little Arabella Miller	●				
Little Sacka Sugar			●		●
Mary Had a William Goat		●			●
Michael Finnegan	●			●	
The Name Game	●		●		●
The Old Gray Horse	●	●			●
Old Molly Hare	●	●			●
Once an Austrian Went Yodeling	●				●
The Pawpaw Patch		●			
Plinker Plunker Strummer Zummer Beeper Booper		●	●	●	●
Sarasponda		●			●
Somebody Stole My Hoo-To Foo-To BAH!			●		●
What Have You Seen?	●				
Whosery Here?	●			●	
Willoughby, Wallaby, Woo	●	●	●		

Apples and Bananas

Traditional
Arranged by John Sauls, Jr.

2. I like to ate, ate, ate,
   Ape-ples and ba-nay-nays;
   I like to ate, ate, ate,
   Ape-ples and ba-nay-nays;

3. I like to eat, eat, eat,
   Ee-pples and bee-nee-nees;
   I like to eat, eat, eat,
   Ee-pples and bee-nee-nees;

4. I like to ite, ite, ite,
   I-pples and bi-ni-nis;
   I like to ite, ite, ite,
   I-pples and bi-ni-nis;

5. I like to oat, oat, oat,
   O-pples and bo-no-nos;
   I like to oat, oat, oat,
   O-pples and bo-no-nos;

6. I like to oot, oot, oot,
   Oo-pples and boo-noo-noos;
   I like to oot, oot, oot,
   Oo-ples and boo-noo-noos;

Repeat first verse.

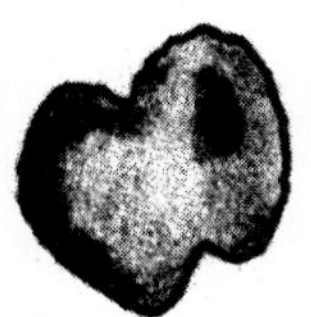 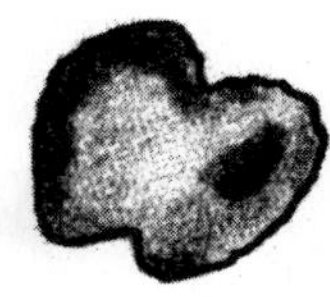 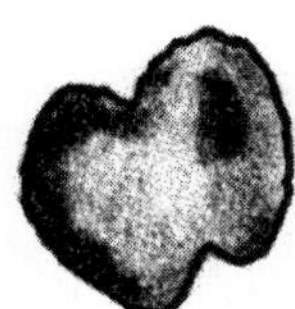 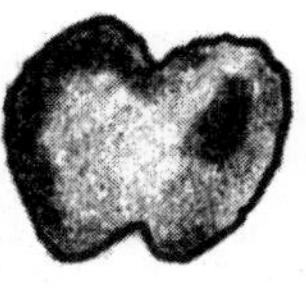 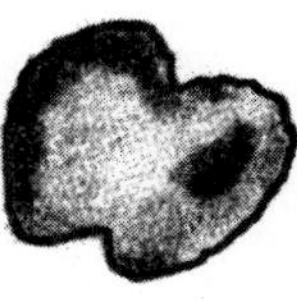 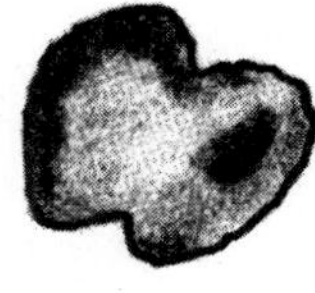

A Ram Sam Sam

Folk Song from Morocco
Arranged by John Sauls, Jr.

BARNYARD SONG

Kentucky Mountain Folk Song

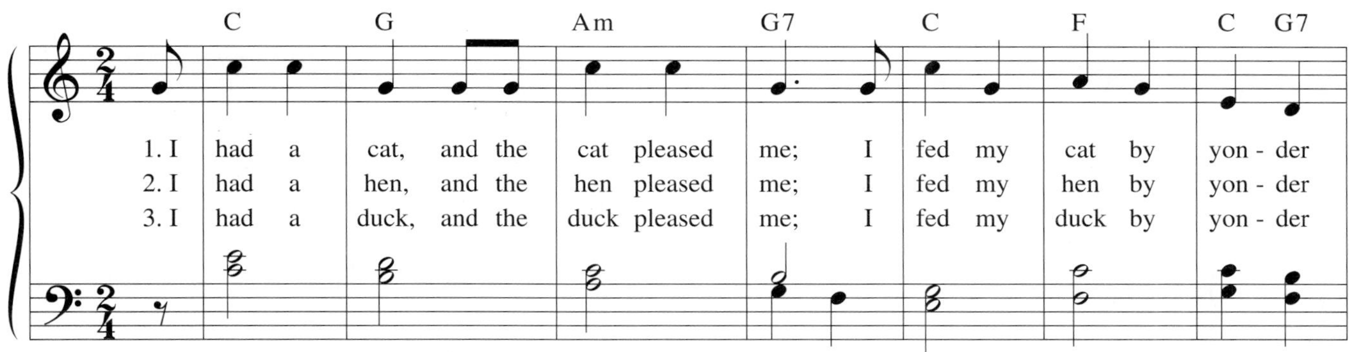
C G Am G7 C F C G7
1. I had a cat, and the cat pleased me; I fed my cat by yon - der
2. I had a hen, and the hen pleased me; I fed my hen by yon - der
3. I had a duck, and the duck pleased me; I fed my duck by yon - der

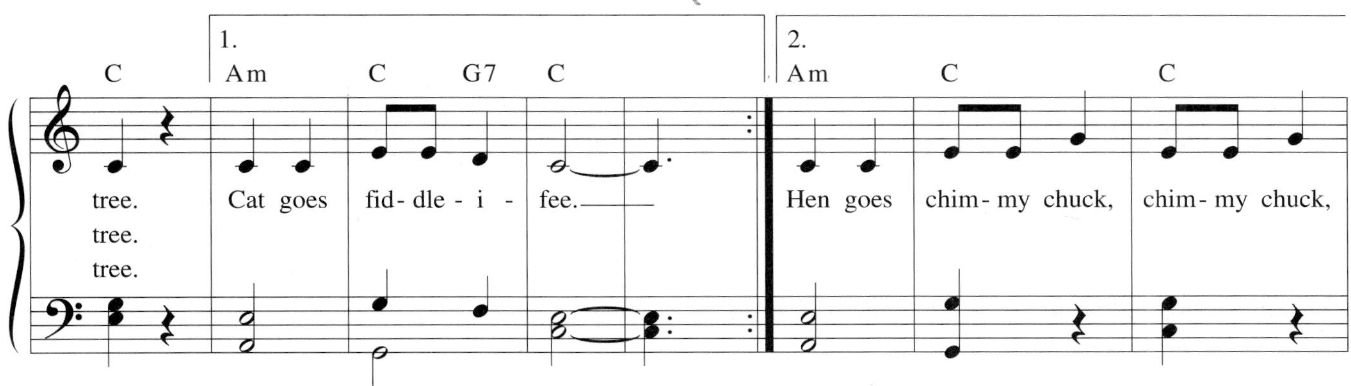
1. 2.
C Am C G7 C Am C C
tree. Cat goes fid - dle - i - fee.
tree.
tree.
Hen goes chim - my chuck, chim - my chuck,

3.
Am C G7 C Am C C
Cat goes fid - dle - i - fee.
Duck goes quack, quack,

Am C C Am C G7 C
Hen goes chim - my chuck, chim - my chuck, Cat goes fid - dle - i - fee.

Add more verses by using goose, sheep, hog, cow, horse, and dog.

Bibbidi-Bobbidi-Boo

(From Walt Disney's "CINDERELLA")

Words by JERRY LIVINGSTON
Music by MACK DAVID and AL HOFFMAN

Brightly

F

Sa - la- ga- doo- la men- chic- ka boo- la

f *decresc.* *f* *mp*

C7 F C7

bib- bi- di- bob- bi- di- boo Put 'em to- geth- er and what have you got bib- bi- di- bob- bi- di- boo.

F C7

Sa- la- ga- doo- la men- chic- ka boo- la bib- bi- di- bob- bi- di- boo. It- 'll do mag- ic be- lieve it or not,

mp

F Bb F Dm
bib- bi- di- bob- bi- di- boo. Sa- la- ga- doo- la means men-chic- ka boo- le- roo, But the
mf
G7 Dm7 Bbm G7 C7 Gm7 C7 F
thing- a- ma- bob that does the job is bib - bi- di- bob- bi- di- boo. Sa- la- ga-doo- la men-chic-ka boo-la
cresc.
mp
C7
bib - bi - di - bob - bi - di - boo Put 'em to - geth - er and what have you got
F
bib - bi - di - bob - bi - di bib - bi - di - bob - bi - di bib - bi - di - bob - bi - di - boo.
f

Burgalesa

Folk Song from Spain

Arranged by John Sauls, Jr.

Moderately

F C7 F C7 F

1. I have two bill - i - rills, Two dol - lar bill - i - rills, And twen - ty nick - el - els That I can spend, I have a
2. There's a fi - es - ta - ra, Such a fi - es - ta - ra, Down at the pla - za - ra, I'll take you there, For this fi -

B♭ F F C7 F

F
B♭
F
cart - a - ra, Such a fine cart - a - ra, Drawn by a
es - ta - ra's, A grand fi - es - ta - ra, The ver - y
C7
F
mule - a - ra, Hop in, my friend.
best - a - ra, found an - y where.

Clickety-Clack
Words and Music by Charles Harvey
1. Click - et - y - clack, a - lunk, a - lunk! A train is com - ing, a - chunck, a - chunck; A click - et - y - clack a mile a - way; It has - n't a sec - ond o' time to stay; It sings a noi - sy clack - et - y song, A rick - et - y, rock - et - y, rack - et - y song, "You're on the track, get out of the way, go 'long!"
2. O - ver the bridge, a - cross the lake, A mile a min - ute it has to make; A ter - ri - ble snake, with flam - ing eyes, That wig - gles and wrig - gles a - long the ties, The cin - ders fall in fi - er - y rain, A tun - nel is wait - ing to swal - low the train, Good - bye, good - bye! To - mor - row he'll come a - gain!

The Corner Grocery Store

Traditional
Adapted Lyrics by Raffi and D. Pike

Moderately
No chord
F
1. There was cheese, cheese, walk - in' on its knees, In the
(2. There were) plums, plums, twid - d - ling their thumbs, In the
mf
C
F
store, in the store. There was cheese, cheese,
store, in the store. There were plums, plums,
1., 2., 4. to Chorus
C7
F
B♭/F
walk - in' on its knees, In the cor - ner gro - cer - y store.
twid - d - ling their thumbs, In the cor - ner gro - cer - y store.
My
last time ritard.

3. There was corn, corn,
 blowin' on a horn,
 In the store, in the store.
 There was corn, corn, blowin'
 on a horn,
 In the corner grocery store.
 (to Verse 4)

4. There were beans, beans,
 tryin' on some jeans,
 In the store, in the store.
 There were beans, beans,
 tryin' on some jeans,
 In the corner grocery store.
 (to Chorus)

5. There was more, more, just
 inside the door,
 In the store, in the store.
 There was more, more, just inside
 the door,
 In the corner grocery store.
 (to Fine, end without Chorus)

Down by the Bay

G7
ev - er see a goose, kiss - ing a moose, Down by the
1.
C no chord
2.
C
bay? Down by the bay?

2. Down by the bay, where the wa-ter-mel-ons grow,
   Back to my home, I dare not go,
   For if I do, My moth-er will say . . .
   Did you ev-er see a whale, with a pol-ka dot tail,
   Down by the bay?

3. Down by the bay, where the wa-ter-mel-ons grow,
   Back to my home, I dare not go,
   For if I do, My moth-er will say . . .
   Did you ev-er see a fly, wear-ing a tie,
   Down by the bay?

4. Down by the bay, where the wa-ter-mel-ons grow,
   Back to my home, I dare not go,
   For if I do, My moth-er will say . . .
   Did you ev-er see a bear, comb-ing his hair,
   Down by the bay?

5. Down by the bay, where the wa-ter-mel-ons grow,
   Back to my home, I dare not go,
   For if I do, My moth-er will say . . .
   Did you ev-er see llamas, eat-ing their pa-jam-as,
   Down by the bay?

6. Down by the bay, where the wa-ter-mel-ons grow,
   Back to my home, I dare not go,
   For if I do, My moth-er will say . . .
   Did you ev-er see an octopus, danc-ing with a pla-ty-pus,
   Down by the bay?

7. Down by the bay, where the wa-ter-mel-ons grow,
   Back to my home, I dare not go,
   For if I do, My moth-er will say . . .
   Did you ev-er have a time, when you couldn't make a rhyme,
   Down by the bay?

Eletelephony
Words by Laura Elizabeth Richards
Music by Jane Hart
With clarity
Once there was an el - e - phant, Who tried to use the
tel - e - phant– No! No! I mean an el - e - phone Who tried to use
the tel - e - phone (Dear me, I am not
cer - tain quite That e - ven now I've got it right.)

D
Em
How - e'er it was, he got his trunk En - tan - gled in the
Em
G
D
D7
tel - e - phunk; The more he tried to get it free, The lou - der buzzed the
G
B7
Em
tel - e - phee The more he tried to get it free, The
F♯
Bm
Em
lou - der buzzed the tel - e - phee (I fear I'd bet - ter drop the song Of
G
A7
D
el - e - phop and tel - e - phong!)

FOOBA-WOOBA JOHN

Jazzy

B♭ Gm F7 B♭ E♭ B♭ E♭

1. Saw a flea kick a tree, Foo - ba - woo - ba, foo - ba - woo - ba,
2. Saw a frog chase a dog, Foo - ba - woo - ba, foo - ba - woo - ba,

B♭ Gm F7 Gm F7 B♭

Saw a flea kick a tree, Foo - ba - woo - ba John;
Saw a frog chase a dog, Foo - ba - woo - ba John;

Gm F7 B♭ F7 Gm F7

Saw a flea kick a tree In the mid - dle of the sea.
Saw a frog chase a dog Sit - ting on a hol - low log.

B♭
Gm
C7
F7
B♭
Hey, John, ho, John, Foo - ba - woo - ba John.
Hey, John, ho, John, Foo - ba - woo - ba John.

3. Saw a snail chase a whale,
   Fooba-wooba, fooba-wooba,
   Saw a snail chase a whale,
   Fooba-wooba John;
   Saw a snail chase a whale
   All around the water pail.
   Hey, John, ho, John,
   Fooba-wooba John.

4. Heard a cow say me-ow,
   Fooba-wooba, fooba-wooba,
   Heard a cow say me-ow,
   Fooba-wooba John;
   Heard a cow say me-ow,
   Then I heard it say bow-wow.
   Hey, John, ho, John,
   Fooba-wooba John.

The Frog in the Well

Folk Song from the Southern Appalachians
Arranged by John Sauls, Jr.

Lively

G D7 G

1. There was a frog lived
2. The frog went swim - ing

C G D7 G D7

in the spring, Sing song Kit - ty can't you ki - mey O; He
'cross the lake, Sing song Kit - ty can't you ki - mey O; He

G C G D7

was so fat he could not swim, Sing song Kit - ty can't you
got swall - owed by a big black snake, Sing song Kit - ty can't you

G
ki - mey O. (Verses 1. & 2.) Kee - mey O ma ki - mey O ma dir - ey O ma wear, Me
ki - mey O.
D7 G C D7 G D7 G D7
hi, me ho, me in come Sal - ly Sin - gle, Some time Pen - ny Win - kle, In stepped nip cat,
G D7 G D7 G G
1. 2.
Hit him with a brick bat, Sing song Kit - ty can't you ki - mey O. The ki - mey O.

Goin' to the Zoo

By Tom Paxton

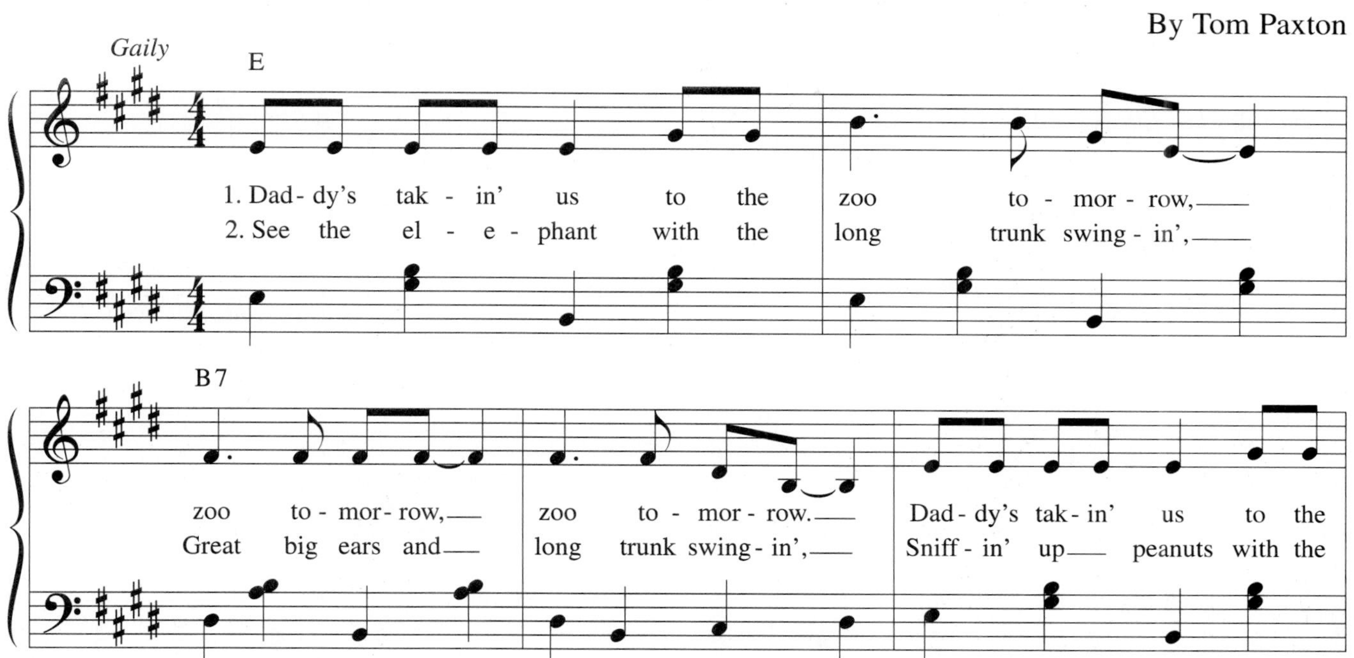
Gaily
E
1. Dad- dy's tak - in' us to the zoo to - mor - row,
2. See the el - e - phant with the long trunk swing - in',
B7
zoo to - mor- row, zoo to - mor - row.
Great big ears and long trunk swing - in',
Dad - dy's tak - in' us to the
Sniff - in' up peanuts with the

ZOO

B7 E

zoo to - mor - row. We can stay all day.

long trunk swing - in'. We can stay all day.

Refrain E A E B7 E A

We're go- in' to the zoo, zoo, zoo. How a- bout you, you,

E B7 E A E

you? You can come too, too, too. We're go- in' to the zoo, zoo, zoo.

3. See all the monkeys scritch, scritch, scratchin',
Jumpin' round scritch, scritch, scratchin',
Hangin' by their long tails scritch, scritch,
scratchin'.
We can stay all day. *Refrain*

4. Big black bear all huff, a-puffin',
Coat's too heavy, he's a-puffin',
Don't get too near the huff, a-puffin'.
You can't stay all day. *Refrain*

5. Seals in the pool all honk, honk, honkin',
Catchin' fish and honk, honk, honkin',
Little seals honk, honk, a-honkin'.
We can stay all day. *Refrain*

6. We stayed all day, and I'm gettin' sleepy,
Gettin' sleepy, gettin' sleepy,
Home already, and I'm sleep, sleep, sleepy.
We have stayed all day. *Refrain*

Hanstead Boys

Folk Song from Nova Scotia
Words adapted by Barbara Andress

C C G
1. The Han - stead boys, they have no sleds. They

G C G C
slide down the hills on the her - ring heads.

2. The Hanstead boys, they have no combs.
They comb their heads with the herring bones.

3. The Hanstead boys, they have no pins.
They mend their coats with old fish fins.

4. The Hanstead boys, they have no nails.
They fix their roofs with old fish scales.

5. The Hanstead boys, they have no pies.
They dine and sup on old fish eyes!

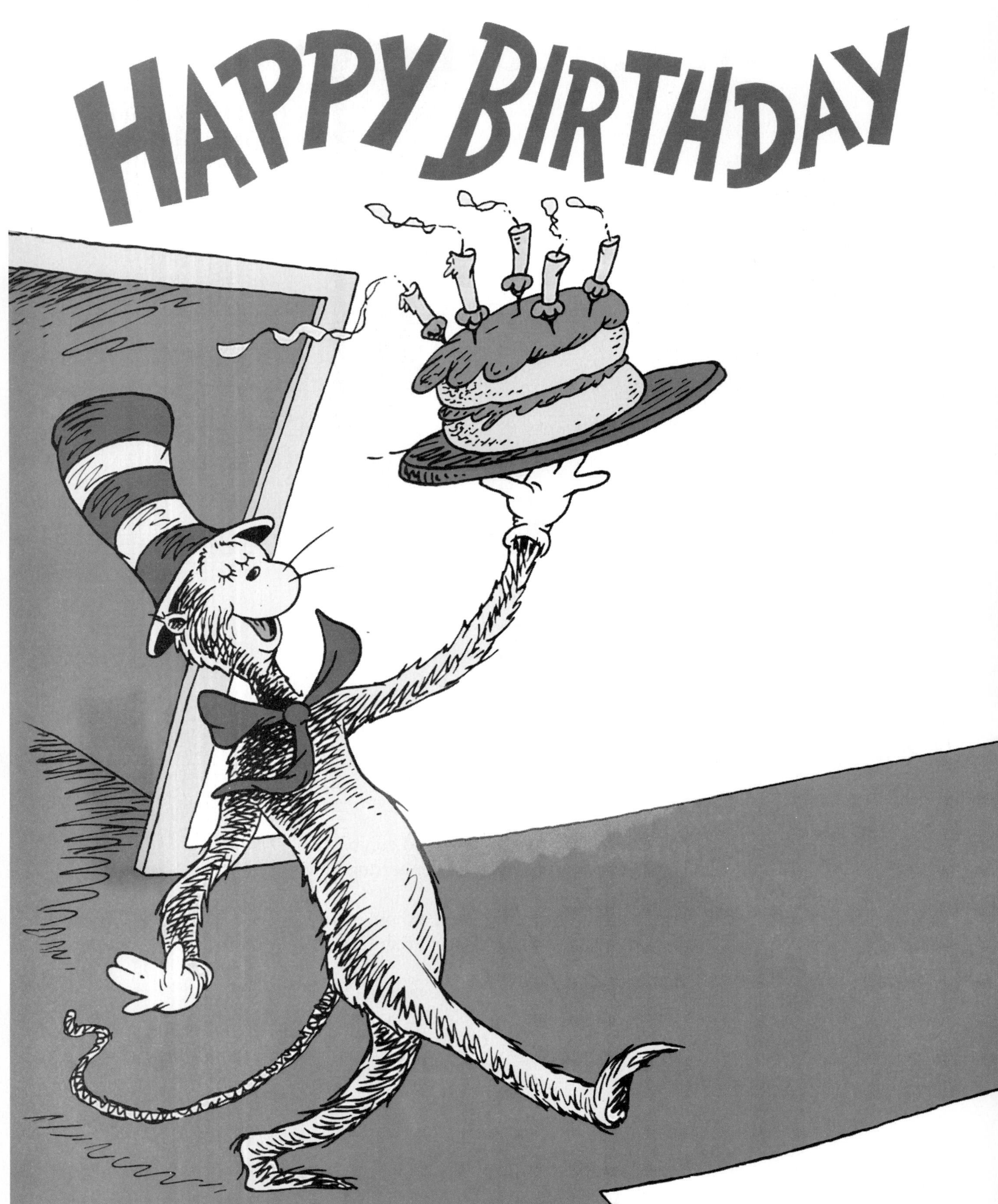
HAPPY BIRTHDAY

To Little SALLY SPINGEL SPUNGEL SPORN

Words by Dr. Seuss
Piano Score and Guitar Chords by Eugene Poddany

With expression

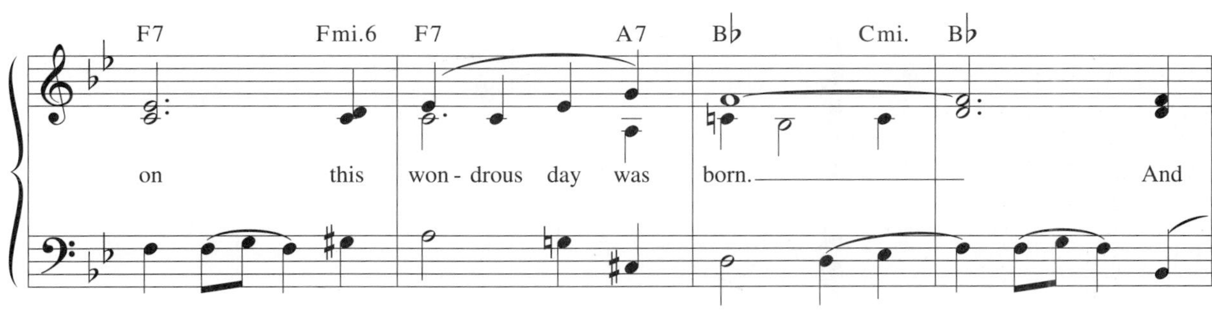

Fred'rick FUTZENFELL
WALDO WILBERFORCE
E♭ E♭dim. E♭ F F9 B♭ A B♭
hap - py birth - day al - so to Fred - ric Futz - en - fell, who was
C Cdim. C7 F C7 F7 F7
born up - on this won - drous day as well. And
B♭ D D7 E♭ G7
hap - py birth - day al - so, to Wal - do Wil - ber - force.

C7 Csus.4 C7 cresc. F ritard. C7 F7
Hap - py birth - day like - wise, to Paul Re - vere's fine horse. But
B♭ D7 Gm. sus.4 Gmi. Gdim.
most of all, we sing to hon - or you
Build up to end
F7 E♭ F7 E♭ F B♭6
spoken
(honored name)
born up - on this great, great,
Cmi.7 F F7 E♭ B♭
8va (like bells)
great day too!
ritard.
Paul's
Horse

His Four Fur Feet

Words by Margaret Wise Brown
Music by Barbara Andress

A7 D Bm

1. Oh he walked a - round the world
2. Then he wad - ed down a stream
3. Then he walked in - to the coun–try
4. He___ walked a - long the riv–er
5. Then he walked___ by the rail–road

on his

Em A7

four fur feet, His four fur feet, His

D Gmaj.7 D A7 D Bm

four fur feet. And he

walked a - round the world on his
wad - ed down a stream on his
walked in - to the coun–try on his
walked a - long the riv–er on his
walked___ by the rail–road on his

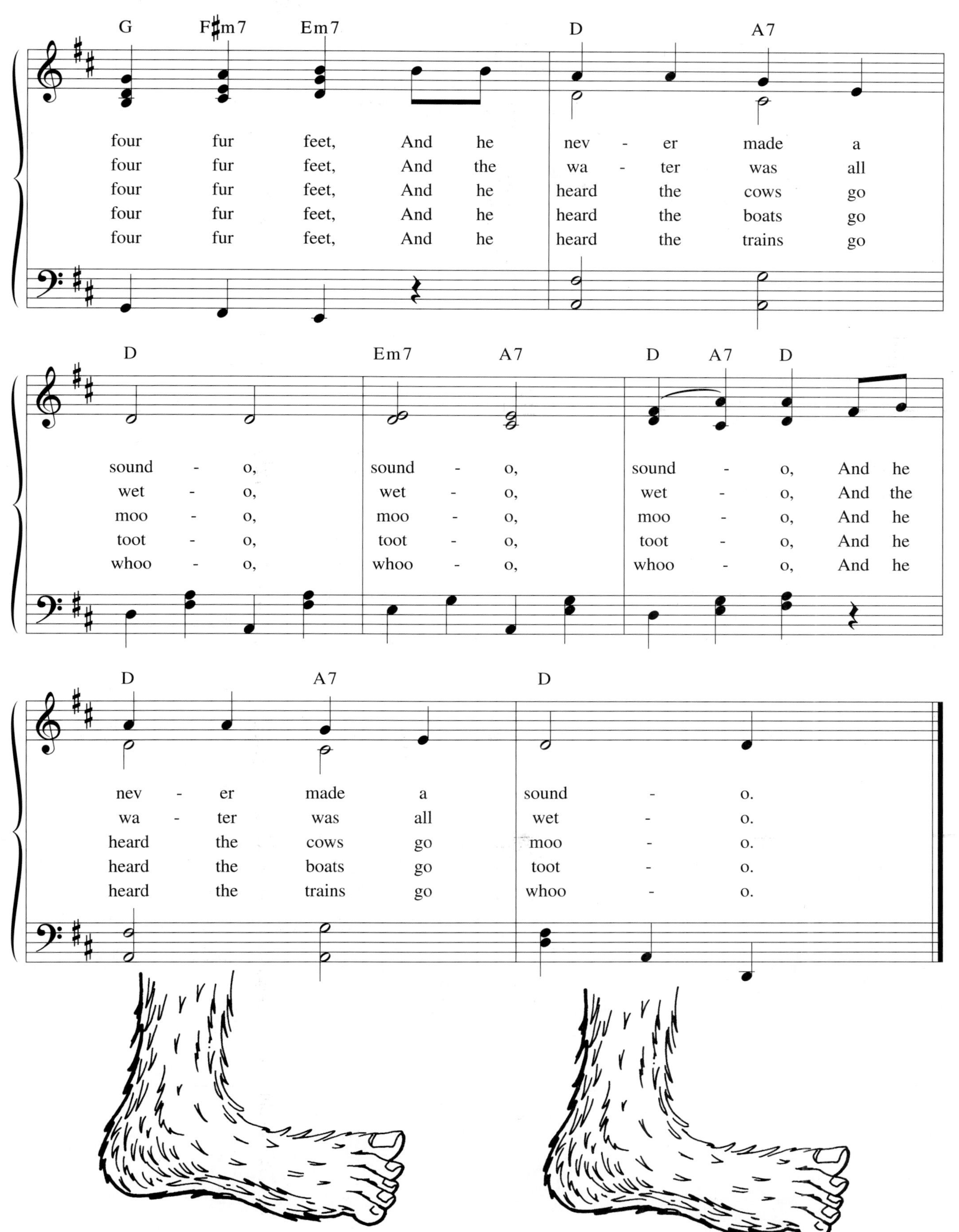
G F♯m7 Em7 D A7
four fur feet, And he nev - er made a
four fur feet, And the wa - ter was all
four fur feet, And he heard the cows go
four fur feet, And he heard the boats go
four fur feet, And he heard the trains go
D Em7 A7 D A7 D
sound - o, sound - o, sound - o, And he
wet - o, wet - o, wet - o, And the
moo - o, moo - o, moo - o, And he
toot - o, toot - o, toot - o, And he
whoo - o, whoo - o, whoo - o, And he
D A7 D
nev - er made a sound - o.
wa - ter was all wet - o.
heard the cows go moo - o.
heard the boats go toot - o.
heard the trains go whoo - o.

HOCKY TOCKY OOMBAH

Camp Song

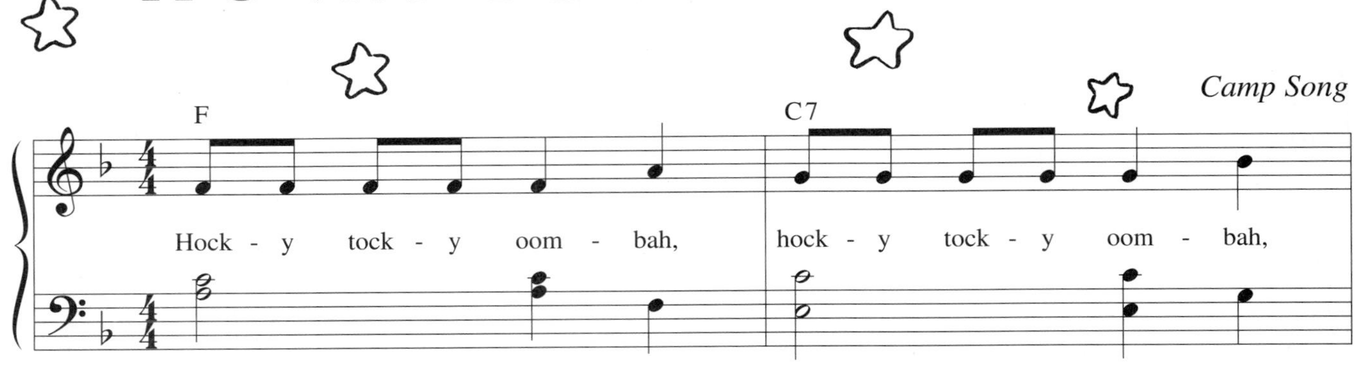
F
C7
Hock - y tock - y oom - bah,
hock - y tock - y oom - bah,

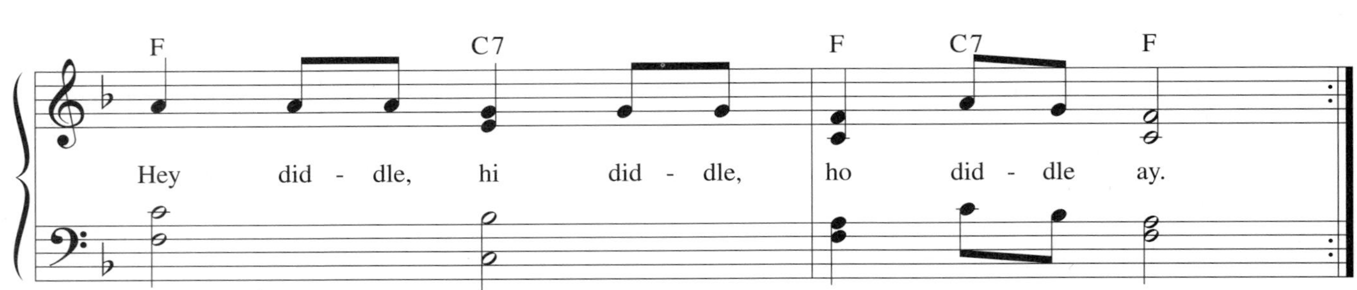
F
C7
F
C7
F
Hey did - dle, hi did - dle,
ho did - dle ay.

Howdido

Words and Music by Woody Guthrie
Arranged by John Sauls, Jr.

Chorus
D7
G
C
N.C.
G
down, how - ji - do.
How - dy doo - zle doo - dle
C
D7
doo - zie how - ji hi - jie hee - jie ho - jie, how - ji ho - jie hee - jie
G
hi - jie, how - ji - do, how - ji - do, how - ji -

C
D7
G
C
G
do sir, doo - dle doo - sie, how - ji - do.

2. And when you walk in my door,
 I will run across my floor,
 And I'll shake you by the hand,
 Howjido, howjido,
 Yes, I'll shake it up and down, howjido.
 (Chorus)

3. On my sidewalk, on my street,
 Any place that we do meet,
 Then I'll shake you by your hand,
 Howjido, howjido,
 Yes, I'll shake it up and down, howjido
 (Chorus)

4. When I first jump out of bed,
 Out my window goes my head,
 And I shake it up and down,
 Howjido, howjido,
 I shake at all my windows, howjido *(Chorus)*

5. I feel glad when you feel good,
 You brighten up my neighborhood,
 Shakin' hands with ev'rybody,
 Howjido, howjido,
 Shakin' hands with ev'rybody, howjido.
 (Chorus)

6. When I meet a dog or cat,
 I will rubby rub his back,
 Shakey, shakey, shakey paw,
 Howjido, howjido,
 Shaking hands with everybody, howdy do.
 (Chorus)

I Make Myself Welcome

F Am F7 B♭ F

1. I'll___ tune up my fid - dle, hi - did - dle - dee - dee; I'll___ tune up my
2. I'll___ play on my tam - bou - rine, jing - a - jing - jing; I'll___ play on my

Dm7 Gm7 (C11) F Fmaj7

fid - dle, hi - did - dle - dee - dee! Oh,___ I can make mu - sic, I
tam - bou - rine, jing - a - jing - jing! Oh,___ I can make mu - sic, I

F7 B♭ B♭m F Dm7 Gm7 (C11) F

play high and low, And I make my - self wel - come wher - ev - er I go.
play high and low, And I make my - self wel - come wher - ev - er I go.

3. I'll___ play on my drum, bum-bum-bum, bum-bum-bum;
I'll___ play on my drum, bum-bum-bum, bum-bum-bum!
Oh,___ I can make mu-sic, I play high and low,
And I make my-self wel-come wher-ev-er I go.

4. I'll___ play on my tri-an-gle, ting-a-ling-ling;
I'll___ play on my tri-an-gle, ting-a-ling-ling!
Oh,___ I can make mu-sic, I play high and low,
And I make my-self wel-come wher-ev-er I go.

5. I'll___ play on my sticks, click-a-click, click-a-click;
I'll___ play on my sticks, click-a-click, click-a-click!
Oh, I can make mu-sic, I play high and low,
And I make my-self wel-come wher-ev-er I go.

6. We'll___ play on our in-stru-ments, go high and low;
We'll___ play on our in-stru-ments, hi-did-dly doh!
We'll___ make our-selves wel-come wher-ev-er we go.
We'll___ make our-selves wel-come, hi-did-dle-dee doh!

I've a Pair of Fishes

Jewish Folk Tune
Words by J. Lilian Vandevere

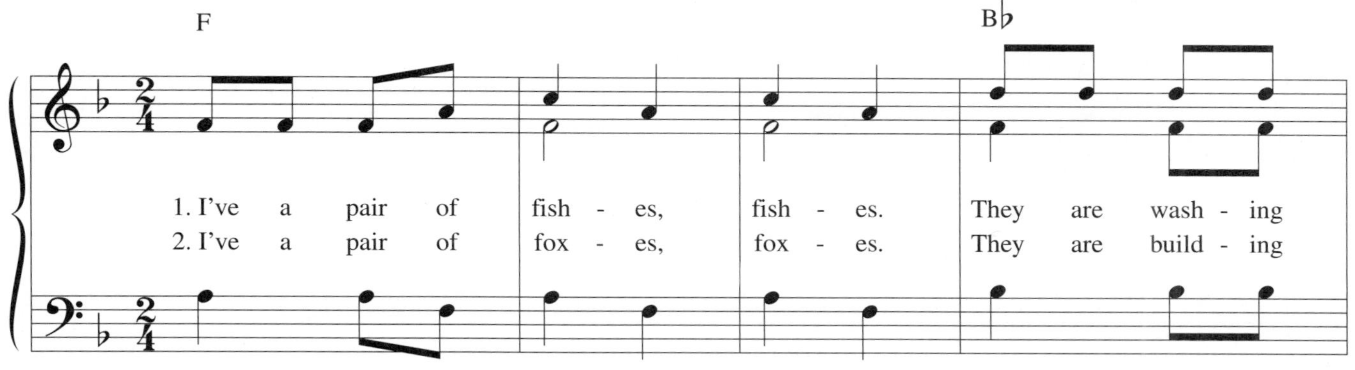
F
B♭
1. I've a pair of fish - es, fish - es. They are wash - ing
2. I've a pair of fox - es, fox - es. They are build - ing

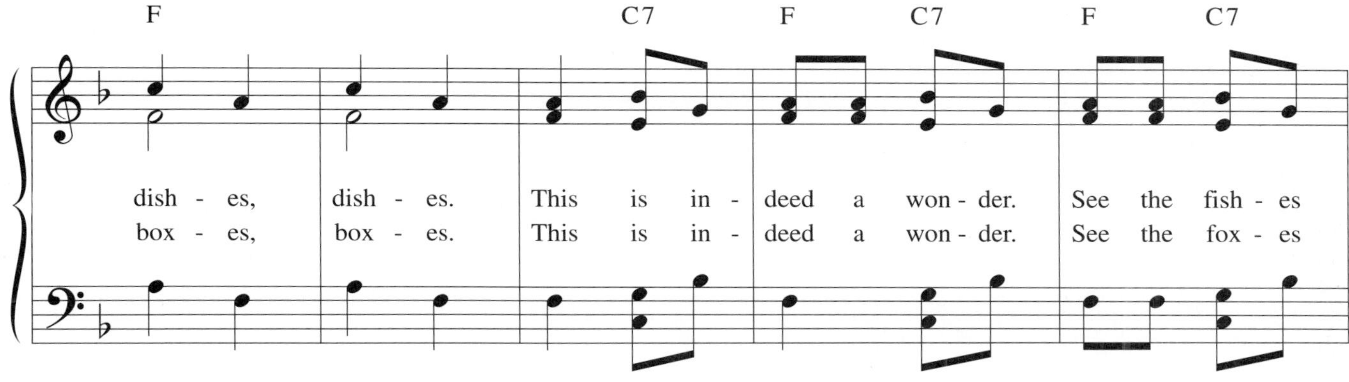
F C7 F C7 F C7
dish - es, dish - es. This is in - deed a won - der. See the fish - es
box - es, box - es. This is in - deed a won - der. See the fox - es

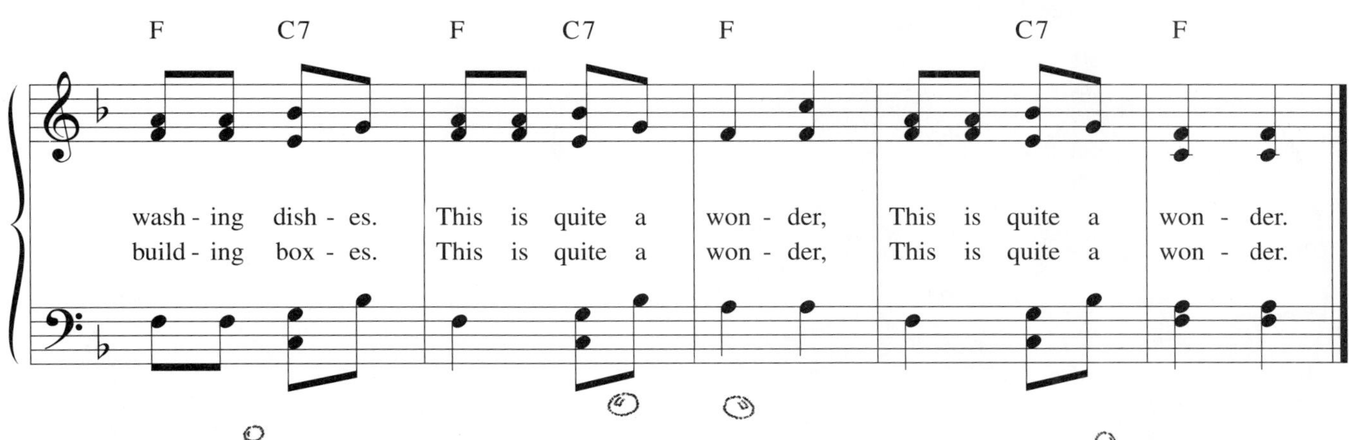
F C7 F C7 F C7 F
wash - ing dish - es. This is quite a won - der, This is quite a won - der.
build - ing box - es. This is quite a won - der, This is quite a won - der.

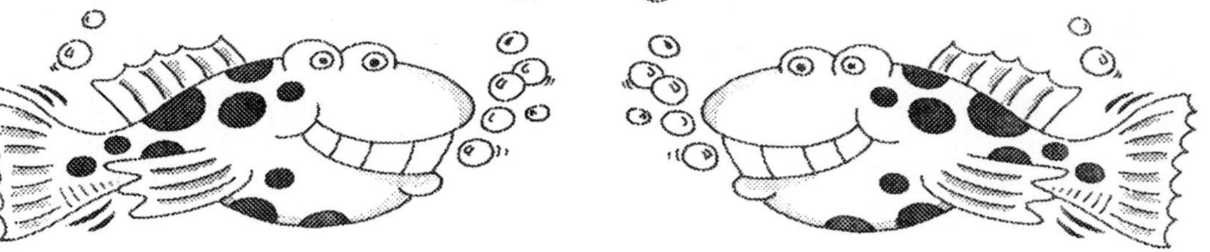

Jennie Jenkins

Early American Song

F Dm B♭ C7 F Dm

1. Will you wear white, O my dear, O my dear? Oh, will you wear white,— Jen-nie

B♭ C7 B♭ F Gm F C7

Jen - kins? I won't wear white, for the col - or's too bright,

Refrain

F Bb B° F

I'll buy me a fol - de - rol - dy, til - de tol - dy, seek - a - dou - ble

Dm Dbaug F C7 F Bb F

roll, ______ Jen - nie Jen - kins, roll. ______

2. Will you wear red, O my dear, O my dear?
   Oh, will you wear red, Jennie Jenkins?
   I won't wear red, it's the color of my head,
   Refrain

3. Will you wear purple, my dear, O my dear?
   Oh, will you wear purple, Jennie Jenkins?
   I won't wear purple, it's the color of a turtle,
   Refrain

4. Will you wear green, O my dear, O my dear?
   Oh, will you wear green, Jennie Jenkins?
   I won't wear green, it's a shame to be seen,
   Refrain

5. Will you wear blue, O my dear, O my dear?
   Oh, will you wear blue, Jennie Jenkins?
   I won't wear blue, for it isn't very true,
   Refrain

Jig Jog Jig Jog

Folk Song
C
1. I want some - one to buy me a po - ny, jig jog jig jog
2. Not too fat and not too bo - ny, jig jog jig jog
Dm G7 C
jig - a jog, gee.
jig - a jog, gee.
F C
For I want to go for a ride
F C D7 G7 C
All a - round the coun - try - side. With a jig jog jig jog,
Dm G7 C
jig jog jig jog, jig jog jig - a jog, gee.

JIM ALONG, JOSIE

With spirit
Traditional
C G C
Hey, Jim a - long, Jim a - long, Jo - sie.
C G7 C
Hey, Jim a - long, Jim a - long, Joe! Hey, Jim a - long,
G C G C Fine
Jim al - ong, Jo - sie. Hey, Jim a - long, Jim a - long, Joe!
C F C
Face to the cen - ter. Hands on your knees.
F C G C D.C. al Fine
Clap three times and turn a - round, please!

The Kangaroo

Chorus

F♯mi. E F♯mi. C♯mi. F♯mi.

Ki - ma-nee - ro kid - dy kum kee - ro, Ki - ma-nee - ro ki - mo,

Bmi. F♯mi. Bmi. A G A Bmi.

Ba - ba - ba - ba bil - ly il - ly ink - um, Ink - um kid - dy kum ki - mo.

3. A kangaroo sat on a bus,
To my ink-um kid-dy kum ki-mo,
Watching a sailor make a fuss,
To my ink-um kid-dy kum ki-mo.
Chorus

4. A kangaroo sat on a path,
To my ink-um kid-dy kum ki-mo,
Watching a tailor take a bath,
To my ink-um kid-dy kum ki-mo.
Chorus

Kitty Alone

Softly flowing
C F G C G C
1. Saw a crow a - fly - ing low, Kit - ty a - lone, kit - ty a - lone;
2. In came a lit - tle bat, Kit - ty a - lone, kit - ty a - lone;
C F G F C
Saw a crow a - fly - ing low, Kit - ty a - lone, a - lye;
In came a lit - tle bat, Kit - ty a - lone, a - lye;

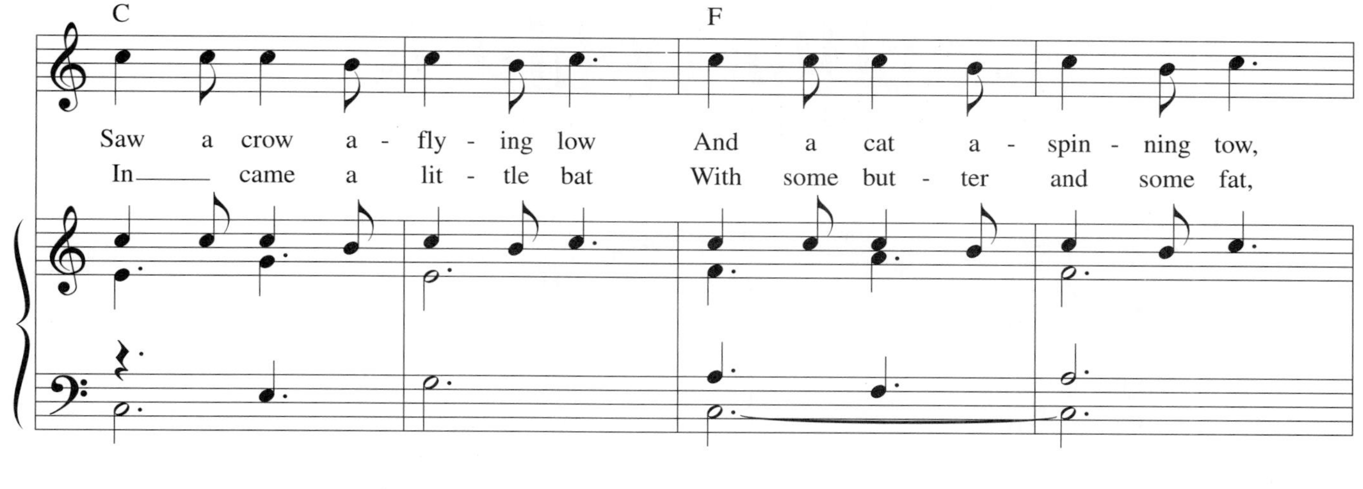
C
F
Saw a crow a - fly - ing low And a cat a - spin - ning tow,
In came a lit - tle bat With some but - ter and some fat,

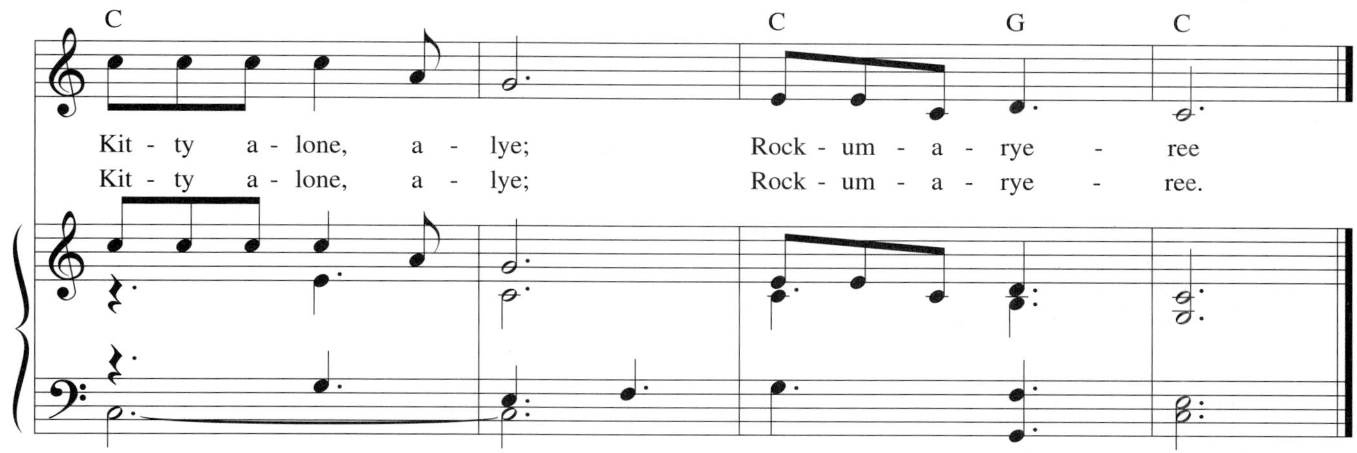
C
C
G
C
Kit - ty a - lone, a - lye; Rock - um - a - rye - ree
Kit - ty a - lone, a - lye; Rock - um - a - rye - ree.

3. Next came in was a honeybee, kitty alone, kitty alone;
   Next came in was a honeybee, kitty alone, a-lye;
   Next came in was a honeybee with a fiddle across his knee,
   Kitty alone, a-lye; rock-um-a-rye-ree.

4. Next came in was little Pete, kitty alone, kitty alone;
   Next came in was little Pete, kitty alone, a-lye;
   Next came in was little Pete fixing around to go to sleep,
   Kitty alone, a-lye; rock-um-a-rye-ree.

5. Bee-o, bye-o, baby-o, kitty alone, kitty alone;
   Bee-o, bye-o, baby-o, kitty alone, a-lye;
   Bee-o, bye-o, baby-o, bye-o, bee-o, baby-o,
   Kitty alone, a-lye; rock-um-a-rye-ree.

Lippity-Lip

Words and Music by Dudley Glass
D
F♯m
G
1. Lip - pi - ty - lip! Lip - pi - ty - lip! Pe - ter Rab - bit
2. Lip - pi - ty - lop! Lip - pi - ty - lop! Pe - ter Rab - bit
D
Em
Em7♭5
D
Bm
went on a trip, Wear - ing a new Jack - et of blue.
nev - er could stop Look - ing for fun, Start - ed to run.
1.
A7
D
Lip - pi - ty, lip - pi - ty - lip!
2.
A7
D
B7
Em
A7
D
Lip - pi - ty, lip - pi - ty, lip - pi - ty, lip - pi - ty - lop!

Little Arabella Miller

Traditional
C F C Dm7 C G7 C
Lit - tle Ar - a - bel - la Mil - ler found a wool - ly cat - er - pil - lar.
Dm G7 C G7 C Dm G7 C G7
First it crawled up - on her moth - er, then up - on her ba - by broth - er;
C F C Dm G7 C G7sus G7 C
All said, "Ar - a - bel - la Mil - ler, Take a - way that cat - er - pil - lar."

Little Sacka Sugar

Words and Music by Woody Guthrie
Arranged by John Sauls, Jr.

E B7

Jig- gle, Jig- gle, Jig- gle, lit- tle tic- kle, tic- kle, tic- kle, tic- kle
(Jig- gle, pick- le, pick- le, pick- le, pick- le,)

E

Lit - tle sack of sug - ar I could eat you up.

Verse:

B7

1. Hey, hey, hey, my lit - tle sack of su - gar,
Hee, hee, hee, my pret - ty lit - tle an - gel,

E
Ho, ho, ho, my lit - tle sack of sweet.
Pret - ty, pret - ty, pret - ty, I could eat your feet.

2. Hey, hey, hey, my little honey bunny,
   Ho, ho, ho, my little turtle dove.
   Hee, hee, hee, my little sack of ’taters,
   So pretty, pretty, pretty, I could eat your toes. *(Chorus)*

3. Hey, hey, hey, my tootsie wootsie,
   Wrangle, tangle, dangle and my honey in a tree.
   Ho, ho, ho, my butterfly fritter,
   So pretty, pretty, pretty I could eat your nose. *(Chorus)*

4. Google, google, google, a coo and a cuddle,
   I kick your foot, like a bicycle pedal;
   Pretty little hoot owl and a one-eyed frog,
   So pretty, pretty, pretty, I could gobble you whole. *(Chorus)*

Final chorus: repeat “Little sack of sugar I could eat you up.”

Mary Had a William Goat

D A D

Ma - ry had a Wil - liam goat, Wil - liam goat, Wil - liam goat,

Chorus: Whoop - dee-doo - den - doo - den - dah, doo - den - dah, doo - den - dah,

A D

Ma - ry had a Wil - liam goat, and he was lined with zinc.

Whoop - dee-doo - den - doo - den - dah,—— doo - den - doo - den - dah.

MICHAEL FINNEGAN

Traditional

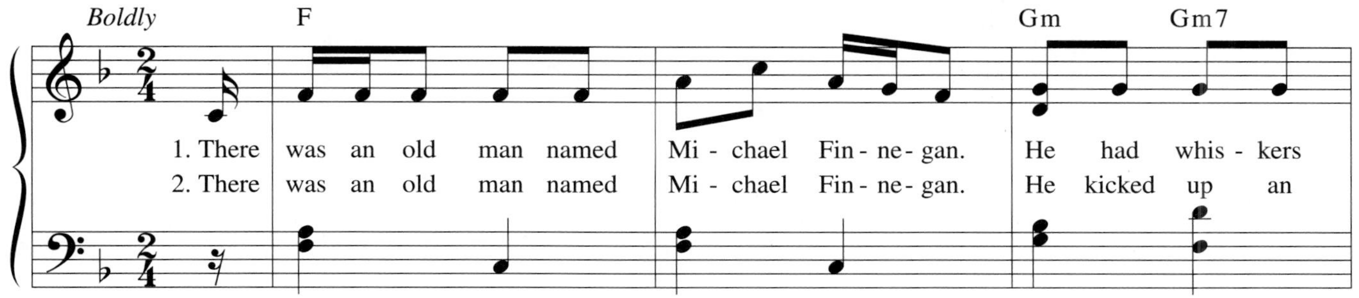

Boldly
F
Gm
Gm7
1. There was an old man named Mi - chael Fin - ne - gan. He had whis - kers
2. There was an old man named Mi - chael Fin - ne - gan. He kicked up an

C
F
on his chin - ne - gan. A - long came the wind and blew them in a - gain.
aw - ful din - ne - gan be - cause they would not let him sing a - gain.

Gm
C7
F
Poor old Mi - chael Fin - ne - gan! Be - gin a - gain.

The Name Game

Words and Music by LINCOLN CHASE and SHIRLEY ELLISTON

With a Bright Beat
mf
The name game.
Shir-ley!
Lin-coln!
mf
F
3
Bb7
Shir-ley, Shir-ley, bo-ber-ley, bo-na-na fan-na, fo-fer-ley, fee fi mo-mer-ley,
Lin-coln, Lin-coln, bo-bin-coln, bo-na-na fan-na, fo-fin-coln, fee fi mo-min-coln,
3
F
F7 F F7 F
Shir-ley!
Lin-coln!
Come on ev-'ry-bod-y, I say now

F7 F F7 F B♭7 B♭ B♭7 B7 F7 F
let's play a game. I bet-cha I can make a rhyme out of an-y-bod-y's name.
F7 F F7 F F7 F
The first let-ter of the name, I treat it like it was-n't there,
F7 F B♭7 F7 F
But a "B" or an "F," or an "M" will ap-pear;
Don
Jan
Sam
Marsha
Billy

F
And then I say "Bo" add a "B" then I say the name, then "Bo -
"Bo" now To-ny with a "B", now "Bo -
F7
Bb7
na - na, fan - na" and "fo." And then I say the name a - gain with an
na - na, fan - na" and "fo." And now you say the name a - gain with an
F7
"f" ver - y plain, then a "fee fi" and a "mo." And then I
"f" ver - y plain, then a "fee fi" and a "mo." And then you
Don
Jan
Sam
Marsha
Billy

B♭7
F7
say the name a - gain with an "M" this time, And there is - n't an - y name that
say the name a - gain with an "M" this time, And there is - n't an - y name that
F
To Coda
F
I can't rhyme. Ar- nold! Ar- nold, Ar- nold, bo- bar- nold, bo -
you can't ryhme. To - ny
B♭7
F
na - na, fan- na fo- far- nold, fee fi mo- mar- mold. Ar- nold! But if the
Don
Jan
Sam
Marsha
Billy

B♭7
F
first two let- ters are ev - er the same, drop them both, then say the name, Like
F
B♭7
Bob, Bob, drop the "B's," Bo- ob, or Fred, Fred, drop the "F's," Fo-red, or Mar-y, Mar - y, drop the
F
D.S. al Coda
"M's," Mo- ar - y. That's the on- ly rule that is con- tra - ry. Say
Don
Jan
Sam
Marsha
Billy

CODA
F
B♭7
To - ny, To - ny, bo - bo - ney, bo - na - na fan - na, fo - fo - ney, fee fi mo - mo - ney,
Bil - ly, Bil - ly, bo - gil - ly, bo - na - na fan - na, fo - fil - ly, fee - fi mo - mil - ly,
Mar - sha, Mar - sha, bo - bar - sha, bo - na - na fan - na, fo - far - sha, fee - fi mo - ar - sha,
F
1–2.
3.
To - ny! Let's do Bil - ly!
Bil - ly! Let's do Mar - sha!
Mar - sha! Lit - tle trick with Nick!
F
B♭7
F
Nick, Nick, bo - bick, bo - na - na fan - na fo - fick, fee - fi mo - mick, Nick!
Don
Jan
Sam
Marsha
Billy

The name game.
Don
Jan
Sam
Marsha
Billy

The Old Gray Horse

Nursery Song
C G7 C
1. Fed my horse in an old wood trough, Fed my horse in an old wood trough,
2. Fed my horse with a sil - ver spoon, Fed my horse with a sil - ver spoon,
3. Fed my horse 'til he got sick, Fed my horse 'til he got sick,
4. Doc - tor said, "He's al - most dead," Doc - tor said, "He's al - most dead,"
G7 C
Fed my horse in an old wood trough, And there he caught the whoop - ing cough.
Fed my horse with a sil - ver spoon, And then he kicked it o–ver the moon.
Fed my horse 'til he got sick, Called for the Doc - tor quick, quick, quick.
Doc - tor said, "He's al - most dead, Put this horse to bed, bed, bed!"
Refrain
G7 C
Koy ma - lin - go, kil - ko, kil - ko, Koy ma - lin - go, Kil - ko kee.

Old Molly Hare

Emi.
Ami.
D
G
"Sit - ting on a hay - stack, Shoot - ing at a bear."
Faster
G
D
G
D
Shack - a - lack - a, shack - a - lack - a, Shack - a - lack - a - shay,
G
D7
G
Shack - a - lack - a, shack - a - lack - a, Shack - a - lack - a - shay.

Once an Austrian Went Yodeling

With great rhythmic emphasis
F
C7
F
1. Once an Aus - tri - an went yo - del - ing on a moun - tain so high, When he
2. Once an Aus - tri - an went yo - del - ing on a moun - tain so high, When he
C7
met with an av - a - lanche, In - ter - rup - ting his cry.
met with a ski - er, In - ter - rup - ting his cry.
Chorus
C7
F
C7
Oh, lay - dee Yo - del - lay - hit - tee, A - yo - del - lay - cuc - koo, cuc - koo,

3. Once an Austrian went yodeling
On a mountain so high,
When he met with a St. Bernard
Interrupting his cry.

Chorus: Oh, lay-dee *(rapid hand-patting of knees, like galloping)*
Yodel-lay-hittee, *(pat–clap–finger-snap)*
A-yodel-lay-cuckoo, cuckoo, *(pat–clap–snap–snap)*
Rumble rumble, *(hands rotate like wheels turning, for avalanche)*
Whoosh! *(hand makes swooping, roller-coaster movement for skier)*
Arf arf, *(hands up in begging position for St. Bernard)*
Yodel-lay-hittee-a-lo.

4. Once an Austrian went yodeling
On a mountain so high,
When he met with a grizzly bear,
Interrupting his cry.
(Continue hand motions in each verse)

Chorus: Oh, lay-dee
Yodel-lay-hittee,
A-yodel-lay-cuckoo, cuckoo,
Rumble rumble,
Whoosh!
Arf arf,
Rargh! *(hands up with fingers like claws in a menacing position, for grizzly bear)*
Yodel-lay-hittee-a-lo.

5. Once an Austrian went yodeling
On a mountain so high,
When he met with a milking maid,
Interrupting his cry.

Chorus: Oh, lay-dee
Yodel-lay-hittee,
A-yodel-lay-cuckoo, cuckoo,
Rumble rumble,
Whoosh!
Arf arf,
Rargh!
Psst psst. *(hands alternate as if milking a cow)*
Yodel-lay-hittee-a-lo.

6. Once an Austrian went yodeling
On a mountain so high,
When he met with a dinosaur,
Interrupting his cry.

Chorus: Oh, lay-dee
Yodel-lay-hittee,
A-yodel-lay-cuckoo, cuckoo,
Rumble rumble,
Whoosh!
Arf arf,
Rargh!
Psst psst,
Eeeeeeeeeeee! *(everyone shrieks wildly and falls on the ground in a heap)*

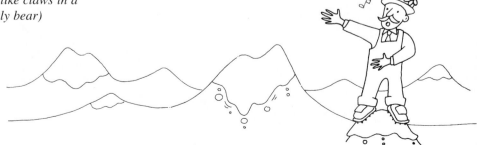

The Pawpaw Patch

Singing Game from Kentucky

Merrily
F
C7
mf
1. Where, oh where is dear lit-tle Mar-y? Where, oh where is dear lit-tle Mar-y?
F
C7
F Bb F
Where, oh where is dear lit-tle Mar-y? Way down yon-der in the paw-paw patch.

2. Come on, boys, and let's go find her,
   Come on, boys, and let's go find her,
   Come on, boys, and let's go find her,
   Way down yonder in the pawpaw patch.

3. Pickin' up pawpaws, puttin' 'em in a basket,
   Pickin' up pawpaws, puttin' 'em in a basket,
   Pickin' up pawpaws, puttin' 'em in a basket,
   Way down yonder in the pawpaw patch.

PLINKER PLUNKER
Words by Dr. Seuss
Piano Score and Guitar Chords
by Eugene Poddany
Brightly
G C Ami. D D7
mf
3
G (PIANO) D7 G
(VOICE)
I can plink a plink- er. Plink! Plink! Plink!
G ritard. Ami. Bmi. G G7
I can plunk a plunk- er. Plunk! Plunk! Plunk! So,

a tempo
C G C G C♯7 D7 B
if you need a fel - low who can plunk and plink, I'm the
Emi. C G A9 (single notes D) D7 G
plunk - plunk plunk - er that you need! Plink, plink!
ritard.
C G7 G♯+ Ami. D D7
spoken
Plink - plink! Plunk - plunk! Plink - Plink, plink!
STRUMMER
ZUMMER

a tempo
G
Ami.
G
Slower
D7
Cdim.
G
(Sing)
I can strum a strum - mer. Strum, strum, strum!
(VOICE)
a tempo
G
Gsus.4
G
Slower
(single notes only)
G7
I can zum a zum - mer. Zum, zum, zum! So,
a tempo
C
G
C
G
C♯7
D7
B
if you need a fel - low who can zum and strum, I'm the
Emi.
C
G
A9
ten.
(single note D)
D7
G
zum - zum zum - mer that you need! Strum, strum!
C
G7
Ami.
ritard.
D
D7
spoken
Strum - strum, zum - zum, strum, strum, strum . . . . !

BEEPER
BOOPER
a tempo
G Ami. G Ami. G Ami. G
(single)
8va
I can beep a beep - er. Beep, beep, beep!
G Ami. G
(single)
ritard
G7
I can boop a boop - er. Boop, boop, boop! So,
a tempo
C G C G C♯7 D7 G B7
if you need a fel - low who can boop and beep, I'm the

Emi. C F♯dim. G A9 ten. (single) D D7 G
boop - boop boop - er that you need! Beep, beep!
Slower D G Cdim. G (single) G 7 5 (single)
l.h.
Plunk, plunk! Strum, strum! Boop, boop, plink! I'm the
G accel. Ami. B7 Emi. C D G C G B♭dim.
mf
plunk- plunk- plunk - er! Zum - zum - zum - mer! Beep- beep - beep - er, that you need
D7 G (single)
p
I think!

SARASPONDA

Rollicking
G
DESCANT:
Bun - da bun - da bun - da bun - da bun - da bun - da bun - da bun - da
TUNE:
Sa - ra - spon - da, sa - ra - spon - da, sa - ra - spon - da, rut - sut - sut.
Bun - da bun - da bun - da bun - da bun - da bun - da bun - da bun - da
Sa - ra - spon - da, sa - ra - spon - da, sa - ra - spon - da, rut - sut - sut. A -

C
G
C
G
Bun - da bun - da bun - da bun - da bun - da bun - da bun - da bun - da
do - re - o, A - do - re - bun - de - o, A -
D7
G
D7
G
Bun - da bun - da bun - da bun - da bun - da bun - da Bun.
do - re - bun - de rut - sut - sut, Ah - se - pah - se - o.

SOMEBODY
MY
HOO-TO FOO-TO
BOO-TO BAH
Words by Dr. Seuss
Piano Score and Guitar Chords
by Eugene Poddany
Andante doloroso
Dmi. Gmi. Dmi. Gmi. Dmi. C
mp
Some - bod - y stole my hoo - to foo - to boo - to bah, and I'm ver - y ver - y
Dmi. Gmi.6 Dmi. B♭mi.6
sad. It was the on - ly hoo - to foo - to boo - to bah
A B♭mi.6 Ami. Dmi. Ami.
that I ev - er, ev - er had. I can't do a thing with - out my
with Pedal
p dolente

STOLE MY HOO-TO FOO-TO BOO-TO BAH!

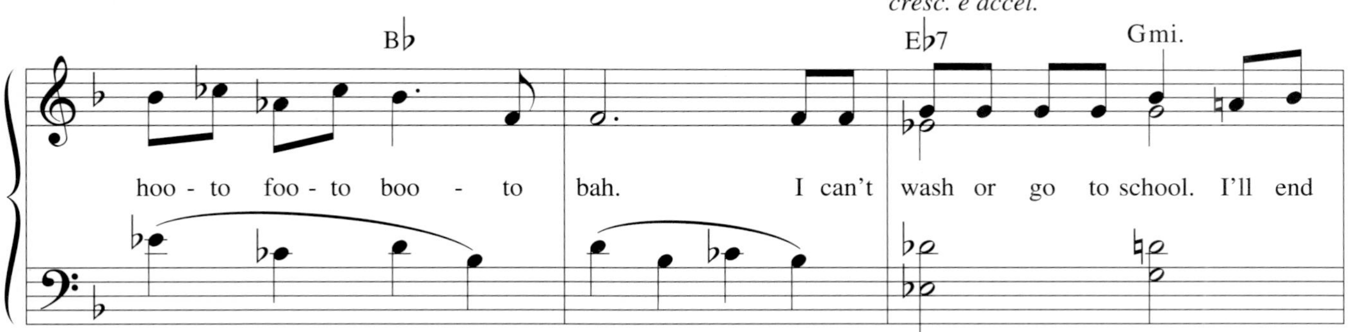

What Have You Seen?

French Folk Song
Arranged by John Sauls, Jr.

Lively Em
Tell us what you saw,
B7 Em B7
On the way to town; Tell us what you saw,
Em
Walking up and down.
1. I have seen a
2. I have seen a
3. I have seen a

B7
Em
pig, Dance an I - rish jig.
hen, Writ - ing with a pen.
bear, Dust - ing off a chair.

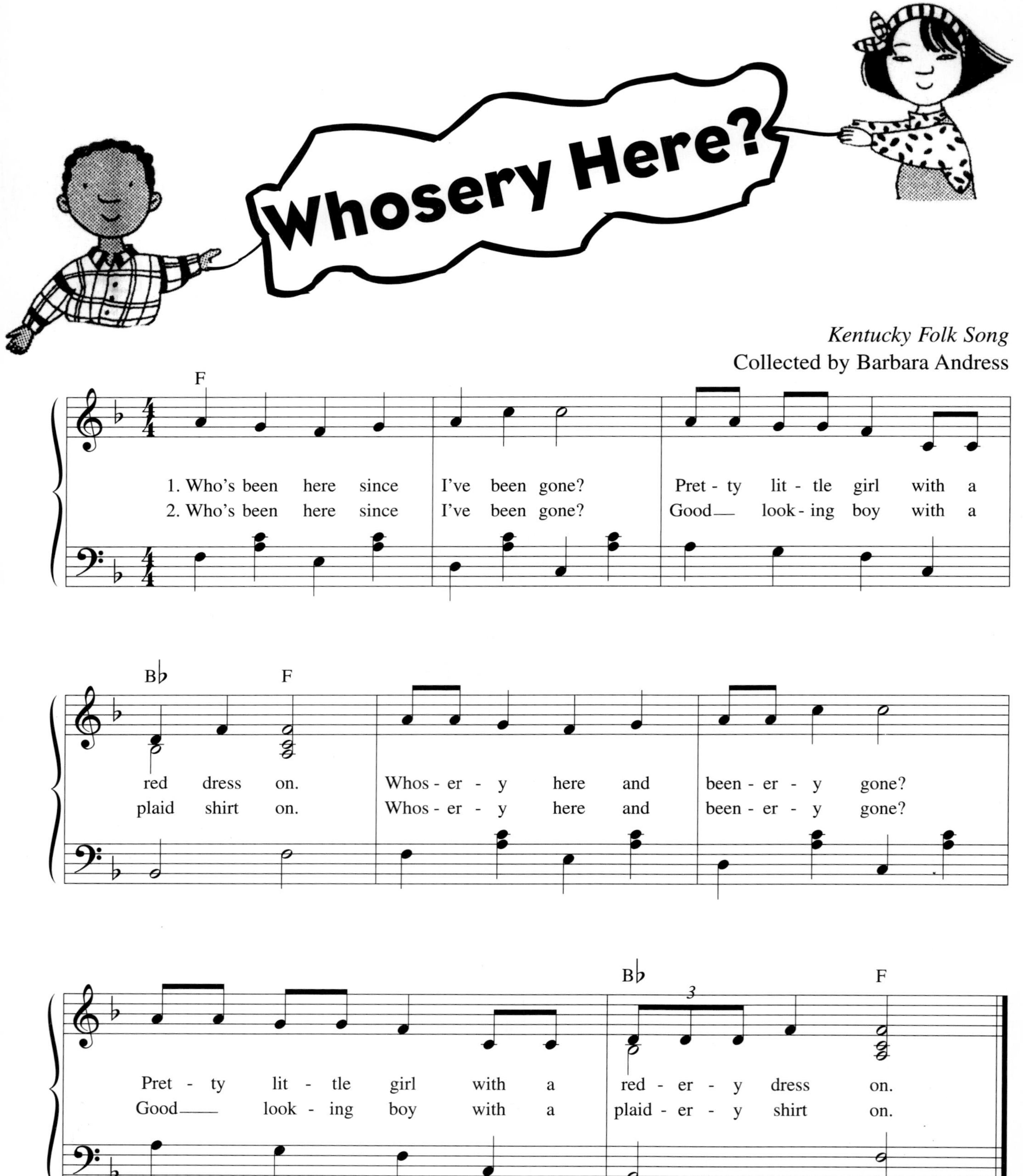
Whosery Here?
Kentucky Folk Song
Collected by Barbara Andress
F
1. Who's been here since I've been gone? Pret - ty lit - tle girl with a
2. Who's been here since I've been gone? Good___ look - ing boy with a
B♭ F
red dress on. Whos - er - y here and been - er - y gone?
plaid shirt on. Whos - er - y here and been - er - y gone?
B♭ F
Pret - ty lit - tle girl with a red - er - y dress on.
Good___ look - ing boy with a plaid - er - y shirt on.

Willoughby, Wallaby, Woo

Larry Miyata/Dennis Lee

2. Willoughby, wallaby wustin,
An elephant sat on Justin!
Willoughby, wallaby wody,
An elephant sat on Cody!

3. Willoughby, wallaby wanny,
An elephant sat on Nanny!
Willoughby, wallaby wen,
An elephant sat on Ken!